"Creating Prospect Attraction"

IDENTITY BRANDING

Revisited...

distinct or extinct

Insurance and Financial Advisors Edition

by **Robert E. Krumroy**

IDENTITY BRANDING

©2000, 2005 by Robert E. Krumroy

Given the current legal environment, we suggest that you consult your compliance or legal advisors before adapting the ideas presented in this book. We have not intentionally included any advice or materials that put you at risk, but we also realize how quickly and often laws and regulations change regarding the financial services industry.

This publication is designed to provide accurate and authoritative information in regard to the subject matter covered. It is sold with the understanding that either the author or the publisher is engaged in rendering legal, accounting, or other professional service. If legal advice or other expert assistance is required, the services of a competent professional person should be sought.

From a Declaration of Principles jointly adopted by a committee of the American Bar Association and a Committee of Publishers.

Michelle J. Polczynski, Design Consultant

I-B Publishing, Greensboro, NC
ISBN: 0-9678661-3-8

Dedication

Dedicated to the financial sales professional, whose long-term success and personal career satisfaction has been built on a foundation of "giving" and not "getting." Whose focus of giving value and enhancing the lives of those they touch has been extended not only to their clients but, also, to their entire community. This professional's commitment to "giving" has established them as the Identity Brand within their local market and has rewarded them with continuous access to prospect communities that welcome their presence. It is this sales professional that stands as a role model to emulate, and the subject matter to which this book is dedicated.

Thank you.

IDENTITY BRANDING

Section 1: The Critical Issues

Section 2: How Did We Get Here?

Section 3: Networking, Finding Prospects and Capturing "Mindshare"

IDENTITY BRANDING

IDENTITY BRANDING

Section 4: How to Get Started

Section 5: Keeping on Track

IDENTITY BRANDING

"Written by a Pro, for the 'Pro' – a must read...offering insights into marketing with unique ideas that can be put to immediate use."

Matt Oechsli, The Oechsli Institute, Author of Winning the Inner Game of Selling

"Creative and distinctive ideas...Strategies that are proven winners for the financial services professional. Cannot help but make you a success!"

Bill Brooks, The Brooks Group, Author of High Impact Selling

"Dizzy Dean said, 'It ain't braggin' if you've done it. Krumroy not only knows what he's talking about, but he's done it!"

Ron Willingham, Integrity Systems, Inc., Author of Integrity Selling

"A marketing pioneer has given us a road map for the future. A must read for any financial professional wanting to survive."

Wallace F. Dale, Database Equity, Inc., Author of Collaborative Database Marketing

" 'Leading edge' ideas on marketing and positioning...should be required reading."

Dennis R. Merideth, CLU, ChFC,
President of the National Association of Insurance and Financial Advisors, 2000-
2001

"Best I've ever read...should be a must for any practitioner."

William D. Pollakov, President-Elect of the General Agents and Managers Association,
2001

"Insightful and impressive...presented to those that are determined to excel, not just survive."

Allan G. Hancock, CLU, ChFC, Past President of the National Association of Life
Underwriters,
past delegate to the White House Conference on Small Business

"For the financial professional seeking long term, meaningful marketplace validation. Ignore his message at your own peril!"

Paul F. Donohue, CRMS, President of MoneyNet

"If you want the 'how to' for becoming known in your market place; becoming an effective CEO of your financial services business...read and digest these insights."

Jack and Garry Kinder, Kinder Brothers International

"Concepts and vision for 'Branding' – accurate, thought provoking, intriguing – goes beyond the basic Madison Avenue drivel. In this new age of competitive warfare and change, this book will show you how to thrive. A must read."

Guy Baker, CLU, MSFS, Top of the Table
Author of Why People Buy, MDRT Foundation President, 2000

"Written for those who want to thrive, a must read...solid advice, examples to model, up-to-the-minute resources...you can gain an almost unfair advantage!"

Pamela Yellen, CEO, Prospecting & Marketing Institute, Inc.

"This book is superb. Someone has finally defined the "illusion" of marketing with logic and clarity. The breadth of EXAMPLES and practical guidelines are priceless...immediately useful for becoming DISTINCT and differentiated in today's competitive marketplace! This is a masterpiece that will redefine the training and focus for sales professionals within the financial services industry."

Charles A. Smith, CLU, ChFC, Executive Vice President and
CEO of the General Agents and Managers Association (GAMA) International

FOREWORD

The revolutionary change in America that Henry Ford caused through mass production is being rivaled by the revolutionary change that consumers are having on how products are purchased and distributed in America. The financial service industry's two primary components for its past success has been focused on developing competitive products and then training or contracting an existing sales force to sell them to the public. In the past, if company revenues began to flatten, products were reviewed to make sure that they were still competitive. If the products proved to be satisfactory, sales systems and sales management were reviewed to discover where the problem was in distribution. Emphasizing quality product features and benefits in conjunction with possessing a proficiency in selling and prospecting skills were the two primary components believed to be necessary for conducting a successful sales encounter. In other words, develop a quality product and find a sales person to deliver it to the customer. I wish sales were still that simple...NO MORE!

The consumer is redefining our formula for success. There is a new discernment that the consumer is applying in making a purchasing decision. That discernment is not predicated on your proficiency in selling or prospecting, but on your proficiency in attraction marketing. Attraction marketing is no longer a skill-module to be mastered after you have been in sales for a period of time. Attraction marketing will become your new business foundation, the universe around which every other system rotates, if you expect to be successful in the future.

Ultimately, this book is about YOU. It's about creating a personal Identity Brand that attracts customers, increases market access, improves your profits, builds prospect attraction and intensifies client loyalty. It is about building a prospect highway to a prospect community and then branding your distinct, unique, intriguing and differentiated personal identity into their minds, which creates a competitive advantage and welcomes your contact. It's what you do to get the customer to notice you first. It's about providing a clear answer to the prospect's question, "Why you?," before ever having a face-to-face encounter.

Before you read this book, I encourage you to answer the following ten questions and then to ponder the answers, some of which may surprise and challenge your current beliefs, but all of which are based on the material in this book. The chapters, thereafter, will provide attraction marketing examples, ways for you to capture "mindshare," practical guidelines for creating market distinction and prospect preference - skills which you must master in the new and very exciting future. The journey is just beginning. Let's get started.

The Ten Question Marketing Checkup

1) Do you believe that focusing training to specific areas such as financial planning, financial profiles, the small business market or long-term care for the over age fifty-five population is attraction marketing?

2) Have you identified a market segment(s) in which you are systematically gathering individual names of prospects (individualized marketing), or have you proclaimed a general market segment in name only, such as the small business market, as your focus?

3) When was the last time you or your manager(s) allocated a significant block of structured time to discuss your attraction marketing strategies to a specific market segment? Is this repeated quarterly? Yearly? Every so often?

4) Do you believe that creating a Web site is part of the answer for meeting the new attraction marketing challenges of the consumer?

5) How does your organization define attraction marketing?

   A) Identifying markets?

   B) Increasing selling skills?

   C) Product development?

   D) Corporate advertising?

   E) Building relationships?

6) Do you believe that providing great service enhances attraction marketing?

7) Do you believe that media or print advertising can create local prospect attraction to you?

8) Do you believe that utilizing direct mail is complementary to your attraction marketing efforts?

9) What are the differences between target selling and target marketing?

10) Do you believe that increasing your national company's name recognition will increase local prospect attraction and sales?

The Ten Question Marketing Answers

1) Training systems and product knowledge, whether advanced or basic, are not components of attraction marketing. Skills and knowledge are very important. If you don't have them, you will find yourself disadvantaged. You will either not be able to deliver what the client expected from your initial encounter or, all things being equal, you will lose the case due to incompetence. You want to be prepared when a selling opportunity exists or when you have an opportunity to talk to a prequalified prospect, but unless you can get into the right doors without having to coerce your way in, you will eventually become the "de-fanged lion," the senior agent with lots of potential but a consistent underachiever. Attraction marketing is about capturing personal "mindshare." It's about building an advantage that opens doors to prospects through creating a superior personal likability and a perception of differentiation, relative to the competition.

2) There are two major components that need to be mastered in order to be successful in sales. They are (1) what to say and (2) to whom to say it. The first skill is the selling skill - how do I get money from the prospect in return for what I am selling? The second skill is the prospecting skill - how do I identify someone who needs what I have to offer and can afford to pay for it? Prospect identification is important, but it is not prospect attraction. There are many sales professionals who belonged to churches or organizations with hundreds of prospects, yet failed in their career. Why didn't they call these hundreds of identified prospects for appointments? Because they knew that consumers viewed their company and themselves as similar to everyone else. Approaches with promises of better performance, service or competitiveness

fall on deaf ears. Without a personal, visible, market distinction, sales professionals are embarrassed to call, fearing more no's than yes's while looking like another Me-Too financial sales professional.

Market access is the number-one problem that keeps people from succeeding or progressing to new heights. If you can't "get in," your skills of prospecting and selling are useless. In order to "get in," you must become differentiated from the consumer's view of parity among your competitors. You need to create a visible distinction, something that is creatively consistent and makes a statement as to who you are, something that attracts the prospect before they have met you. This is called "capturing mindshare." It is the attraction marketing skill.

How do you position yourself to become favorably viewed by the prospect before you have met? You develop an Identity Brand, YOU, and then familiarize the prospect with you through unique experiences in advance of your first personal contact. This can only be successfully accomplished if you have successfully identified and built a name-specific prospect database of people with whom you would like to do business. These names are valued and never lost. Relationships are cultivated with them over time. They are the people you invite to events and to whom you consistently connect. They are the people who make up your *Prospect Fishbowl*™. Once they are individualized, your primary job shifts from finding prospects to seeking opportunities to migrate within their midst. MIGRATION replaces prospecting as your primary focus.

3) Successful attraction marketing requires periodic evaluation of your methods and effectiveness. It begins with a well thought out strategy plan based on creativity and it requires consistent monitoring as to its progress (we would suggest

quarterly). Great marketing is not the result of common sense; it is not working harder; it is not increasing staff to provide more responsive service; it is not about getting better office facilities; it's not about better activity supervision. Effective marketing is about building prospect attraction. It requires doing different things than the competition, rather than doing the same things in different ways. If the competition is going left, you go right. If they are doing X, you do Y. It is about creating a distinct personal uniqueness that is pleasing to your specific market segment. It is created through innovation, not imitation. It is about capturing the entire market, not market share. It requires the allocation of specific thought time directed toward creating a unique and differentiated plan that is action based.

4) Creating your own Web site will not create local prospect attraction. Web sites are validation components. They provide confidence that you are legitimate, but they do not create initial prospect attraction. They will neither open doors to new prospects nor give you a marketing advantage over the competition.

Communication technology will become a growing expectation for building deeper relationships with clients and prospects. You have consumers now who expect you to stay in touch with them through interactive emails. In the future, many will prefer meeting with you through Internet visual-teleconferencing rather than meeting at an arranged location. If you can't accommodate their expectation, they will find someone who can. Get comfortable with electronic communication before you lose out.

Häagen Dazs® Ice Cream currently offers a certificate for one FREE pint of whatever Häagen Dazs product you desire. They request that you fill in your name and email address on the back of the certificate so that they can keep you up to date with "product news, additional coupons and more"...I wonder what "more" means. I wonder what they have in mind. I wonder if they even know. Probably not, but they are smart enough to know that a technology revolution is gripping America with marketing implications we have never experienced. This ice cream company wants your email address! They know that they are going to communicate differently in the future. What are you doing to build an email database that prepares you for the same revolution that even an ice cream company is anticipating?

5) Marketing is the most misunderstood issue in sales today. Most people cannot define the difference between selling and marketing and frequently use the terms interchangeably. The term "market identification" has also been wrongly substituted for the skill of attraction marketing. Consider the owner of a shoe store who identifies the adults in his city who wear shoes, but does not create any distinction that would cause them to buy from him instead of his competition. Shoe prospects may even know his store's name, but if there is no compelling distinction, no visible differentiation, there is no market preference. The shoe prospects will conclude that any store will do; whichever one they encounter first is just fine. Sound familiar? What's your compelling attraction?

Many people think in terms of selling when they think of marketing. You need to have a good selling system, but unless you can gain access to the prospect, you will not be able to apply your selling skills often enough to meet your goals. Additionally, unless the prospect can answer the question, "Why you?," they may not purchase even when you have demonstrated the need and the corresponding solution. "Why you?" is a function of personal relationship building, not your selling proficiency, product or service.

Many home offices think that product development is marketing. After all, they assembled consumer focus groups to get reaction to pre-product development design and then put together the newest product with the best benefits. This may be market-driven product development, but it is not local attraction marketing. It will not affect the issue of "getting in" to see the prospect. It will not improve agent retention, nor will the newest product deliver the senior agent to a market that better matches his or her skill level.

Corporate advertising and promotion is the most sensitive issue to address. To some, it is like attacking mother and apple pie. Corporate advertising does serve a purpose. It can help give the agent credibility at the point of sale. It can provide a comfort level to the consumer who recognizes the company by name. It may be a significant factor in helping to recruit experienced agents or attracting experienced brokers to represent your product. It is helpful in instilling pride in your agents. It is a major factor in the promotion of your stock to the individual investor or the institutional investor and, therefore, helps to maintain a higher stock price. But, corporate advertising does not affect the local agent's ability to "get in" to see the desired prospect.

Attraction marketing is personal, not corporate. It is about capturing local prospect "mindshare." It is about becoming the standard of excellence to a local prospect audience that you will eventually own. It is about becoming personally Identity Branded as distinct from your competition and unique to a name-specific market audience.

6) Giving great service is important and it is expected. Always deliver what you promise. If you don't, you will hamper your client retention efforts and ruin your general reputation among your clients. Negative news is passed along ten times the rate and fifty times the impact that positive news is

passed along. Service is expected and it is important. Service is what keeps clients but it is not what usually attracts new prospects, unless you catch someone fleeing from someone else's bad service experience. Service is not usually an attraction marketing issue.

7) Print or media advertising, even if done in the local market, will not increase accessibility to new prospects. It will not open doors. Print advertising may help increase identification, but it is local brand personality that creates consumer pull and prospect attraction. Building preference starts with an experience. Once you have positively influenced the prospect with enough experiences, you develop "mindshare" or as Guy E. Baker, CLU, ChFC says, you get placed on the "shelf of the mind." It is YOU, your personality, your distinction that you build relative to the marketplace and the corresponding emotional connection that influences the consumer. Unfortunately, print advertising is the most frequently thought of item when people think of marketing. It is the easiest so-called "marketing" item to implement, but it is also the single greatest waste of money that sales professionals ever spend.

8) The United States currently has only six percent of the world's population yet fifty-six percent of the world's advertising dollars are spent in this country. The average consumer is exposed to over 5,000 advertising images per day and receives over 2,200 junk mailings per year. Product proliferation is at an all-time high. People have less discretionary time and are more frustrated with the propaganda and the intrusion marketing methods than at any time in history. Getting our mail is no longer a pleasant experience. It is a daily intrusion on our time. Direct-response-mail campaigns are not building good will. Their strategy is based on an antiquated selling model and not on an attraction-marketing model.

9) Many agents believe that marketing is synonymous with conducting occasional seminars. Just conducting occasional seminars with the idea of selling some of the attendees is not target marketing, neither is it attraction marketing, it is target selling. Holding consistent seminars (once a month, quarterly, etc) that can be identified by your local prospect audience, whether they attend or not, is attraction marketing. To be regarded as marketing, your seminar needs to be focused on building your local market distinction, relative to the competition. Seminars can be one of the elements of a structured marketing plan; developed to create positive experiences for your individualized market segment through consistent familiarity with the same invited audience. Doing occasional or one-time seminars to create sales will never build market distinction, neither will they build a prospect highway to a prospect community.

10) National advertising for companies creates greater name awareness. However, national name awareness does not create local market attraction, particularly for an intangible, infrequently used product. It will not have an effect on creating easier local market access to the prospect. National name recognition is not what creates local consumer attraction, local brand personality does. Brand personality is built through positive experiences at the local level with the advisor. These experiences need to be unique, high in value, memorable and differentiated from the market competition. Consumers in the financial service's market, rarely if ever purchase their intangible, financial product because of a national name. They buy on what they perceive is the superior "package of value" in their local market. That package of value is based on emotional bonds that you have built through the process of creating continual familiarity with you...the real Identity Brand.

IDENTITY BRANDING

IDENTITY BRANDING

The Critical Issues

IDENTITY BRANDING

Innovation – Not Imitation
First – Not Better
Perception Depth – Not Product Breadth
Market Ownership – Not Market Share
Creativity – Not Duplication
It's YOU – Not The Company

Become Distinct or...Extinct

We are entering a marketing revolution, a revolution that will shift market share, a revolution that will displace the previous success of even some of the most experienced sales professionals, a revolution, that if overlooked, will leave you wondering where to find a new prospect.

Something in the marketplace is changing dramatically. If it takes you much longer to identify the winds of change and to respond accordingly, it will be too late. The damage will be irreversible. Even the successful sales professional who was once noted for only working with referrals is struggling. The success of getting a referral to answer their telephone, just to initiate contact, is less than a fifty percent chance as compared to a few years ago when it was almost always successful. Success for these veterans is no longer solely a factor of getting referrals. Neither is getting adequate appointments for succeeding in your business solely dependent on being able to make an effective telephone call for an appointment or on blocking out enough time each week to accomplish the goal.

Don Debelak, author of *Marketing Magic*, says, "Every marketer realizes that customers are becoming increasingly difficult to reach." His suggestion, "...you need to figure out a way for your business to gain a sustainable advantage." If you can't capture the prospect's "mindshare" by creating a personal visible distinction, before the contact is made, your future success will be limited. The sales professionals who want to survive can no longer ignore this market change...NOT THIS TIME!

Ivan R. Misner, Ph.D. and Virginia Devine, authors of *The World's Best Known Marketing Secret,* write, "In today's business environment you need an edge. This means that you need to be very creative in order to be competitive in today's marketplace. Creativity in marketing your [local business] image has become a basic tenet for today's successful company or professional practice." Bernd H. Schmitt, the founder and director of Columbia's Marketing Management Executive Program and author of *Experiential Marketing* concurs. He writes, "Today, customers take functional features and benefits, product quality and a positive brand [name] image as a given. What they want is product, communications and marketing campaigns that dazzle their senses, touch their hearts and stimulate their minds. They want all of this to deliver an experience."

Your national home office can't deliver this. You cannot nationally brand an infrequently used intangible service the same way that you can brand a frequently consumed product such as Coca-Cola® and create local customer attraction. Neither can the local sales professional achieve the same level of perceived quality guarantee from traditional advertising that a consumable product can attain. The customer knows that quality guarantee has far more to do with the local sales professional than it does with the national company name.

What the customer is asking for is locally driven. It's all about branding your personal identity to your local market segment in a visibly unique way. In the near future, those who create a local Identity Brand through consistent familiarization in concert with locally driven, memorable, distinct and unique experiences as compared to the competition will own the prospect. It is not one or the other, but both that will capture the mind of the consumer and provide a competitive edge in selling as well as securing appointments with prospects.

The challenge of your future in the local market place is to become DISTINCT, and not EXTINCT. Chasing the competition with a focus on doing it better or giving better service will be a losing strategy. Local attraction marketing can no longer be a fringe consideration for successful sales professionals. Creating a distinct local market identity within your local market segment will become the most major component within your business. It will dictate the extent of your success in the future.

"You're involved in something BIG: the shift to an entirely new economy…a new age…We jeopardize our future if we cling to old assumptions and expectations…" writes Price Pritchett in *New Work Habits For A Radically Changing World.* Marketing in the 21st century will require a strategy transition. Success will require redirecting your primary focus from getting the prospect to buy to focusing on creating local prospect attraction, delivering YOU as a distinct and unique "package of value," a package of value that is superior to what the local competition, or a direct company contact could possibly offer. How well you (not your national company) do in personally

YOU are a distinct and unique "package of value"…

creating a local superior value perception that creates local customer attraction, before you have met them, will determine your future success. Creating a distinct and differentiated local market presence is the only skill that will give you continued and welcomed access to new prospects and provide the continued stream of activity needed to meet your business and financial goals. It is the only appeal that will influence the customer and convince them to allow you to fit into their picture in this "radically changing world…an entirely new economy."

The competitor who is quicker at creating a superior local prospect perception of distinction and differentiation will become your greatest obstacle to surviving tomorrow's complex, competitive marketplace. Having the best product or the highest level of expertise will not be factors in winning over the prospect's mind or in creating a competitive advantage when trying to get in to see the new prospect. The key to your future success will be in attaining continued welcomed access to new prospects within your market who perceive that you are the "mark of excellence – the preferred choice" BEFORE they have ever met you.

Al Ries and Jack Trout write in *Positioning – The Battle For Your Mind*, "Positioning is not what you do to a product. Positioning is what you do to the mind of the prospect." The job will not be to identify groups of potential prospects and figure out ways to convince them to buy your product. The job will be to create an attraction marketing model that attracts the attention of the local prospect and leaves a lasting impression, one of superior value, on their mind. Regis McKenna, author of *Relationship Marketing*, says, "Marketing today is not a function; it is a way of doing business. Marketing is not a new ad campaign or this month's promotion. Marketing has to be all pervasive, part of everyone's job description, from the receptionist to the board of directors."

> *The job will be to create an attraction marketing model that attracts the attention of the local prospect and leaves a lasting impression, one of superior value, on their mind.*

According to Al Ries and Jack Trout in *Positioning – The Battle For Your Mind*, "Today's marketplace is no longer responsive to the strategies that worked in the past. There are just too many products, too many companies, and too much marketing noise." Positioning is no longer secured by developing product or service superiority. It is a psychological sale of perception. Attraction marketing is a process, not an event. Your personal marketing focus should be on developing prospect attraction and intensifying local market relationships, not just seeking a new sale or order.

Attraction marketing is a process, not an event.

In the future, success will result from becoming effective in creating ongoing dialogue, continuous communication. Your success begins by building a locally visible, superior value distinction that the consumer sees as your Identity Brand, your uniqueness as compared to your competition. Customer preference will not be created through new products, company sent newsletters, Web sites, national corporate name recognition or annual customer survey forms stuffed in annual corporate statements or billings. You will secure your success by Identity Branding YOU. And the more distinctive your personal identity, the greater your appeal to your market audience.

The more distinctive your personal identity, the greater your appeal.

Regis McKenna, author of *Relationship Marketing,* says that unlike the revolutionary products developed in the 1950s and 1960s such as the Weber Charcoal Grill and the color TV, products no longer "suddenly appear in our midst and overwhelm us." Products don't create market positioning when the consumer views them as essentially all equal. McKenna says, "To succeed in the future, marketers will have to learn new and better ways of bringing value to the customer." What actually gets driven into the mind today is not the product. It is YOU, your local image.

market positioning is created in the mind

Personal positioning is no longer the result of selling superior products or offering better service. Personal positioning starts with an experience. For the prospect, that personal experience is the beginning of a perception. This local experience should never be initiated in an opening interview; it should be initiated before the prospect ever meets you. Pre-interview perception is the foundation for establishing an almost unfair competitive advantage, an Identity Brand that outclasses the competition. This foundation is not built out of logic, common sense of working harder. It's built out of creativity.

The following chapters will provide a guide for building this personal positioning foundation - a guide for your future success, leading you through this next marketing revolution while helping you build an Identity Brand, YOU, that eventually becomes the mark of excellence within your local market segment.

I don't know who you are.

I don't know your reputation.

I don't know your business distinction.

I don't know your customers.

I don't know anything about you personally.

I don't know if we share anything in common.

I don't know if I would even like you.

I have no evidence that I should trust you.

Now—what was it you wanted to sell me?

Please hurry. I have important things to do.

MORAL: *The sale starts before your initial call.*

IDENTITY BRANDING

IDENTITY BRANDING

How Did We Get Here?

IDENTITY BRANDING

Marketing Is Misunderstood

Until the 1970's, America was a country that had never felt the effects of inflation. Wages hadn't changed much for over twenty years. People lived in neighborhoods where they not only knew each other but they socialized together. Their children started walking to school together in kindergarten and graduated from high school with those same friends. The new kid in school was a novelty. Very rarely did anyone move. Business was transacted on a handshake. New products took a long time to produce. Infomercials did not exist, most people were buying their first color TV and, prior to 1973, NO ONE had ever received a telemarketing call.

Junk-mail didn't exist; neither did credit cards. Credit was still a novelty, which, if available, was set up with your local men's or women's clothing store that billed you at the end of the month, when, on the rare occasion, you used it. Carhops delivering hamburgers far outnumbered the few McDonald's restaurants that had been constructed. Television had only three channels. There were no remote controls and the TV repairman still came to your home. Divorce was scandalous and rare. Being cheated in a business deal was almost unheard of. The "Ozzie and Harriet" life style was, to a large extent, REAL! But not anymore. You are about to witness the most profound marketing change that has ever affected America. Some will survive. Many will not. Your survival will depend on how well informed you are and the actions that you choose to take. Choose them wisely!

> *You are about to witness the most profound marketing change that has ever affected America.*

The Consumer Wants to Know "Why You?"

Michael Boylan, author of *The Power to Get In,* says, "The rules of the game of getting in have changed drastically. In order to get in the door today, you've got to trash your old strategies, tactics and methods and learn to do things differently." Success is no longer a selling game. It is not even a "let's-find-a-new-prospect" game. It is a prospect attraction game. Attraction marketing is not about strong-arming your way into the prospect's door. It is not even about identifying multiple prospects that need and can afford your offering and then making an effective approach for an initial appointment. It is not about becoming resilient to the first "no," learning the newest answers to objections and then pushing a little harder for a "yes." Attraction marketing is not selling. It is not prospecting. Attraction marketing is about getting the prospect attracted to you before the first contact is initiated. It is about getting prospects to knowingly want you to contact them.

> *Success is no longer a selling game.*

> *Marketing is not selling. Marketing is not prospecting. Marketing is about getting the prospect attracted to you before the first contact is initiated.*

In the professional service industries, the local attraction marketing challenge won't be met through your company's national advertising and promotion campaign. It is a local challenge whose orchestration belongs to you. It is all about how to create a personal local market presence that attracts the prospect and answers their question, "Why you?"

The Prospect Has Changed and Why YOU Will Have to Respond

Marketing is, perhaps, the most misunderstood element in

corporate America today. It is especially misunderstood in the financial service industries that sell intangible products or services that are purchased but not physically used such as insurance, mutual funds, stocks, even accounting and legal services. Many corporate executives argue that their company is different. They send quarterly newsletters, advertise on TV, sponsor national sporting events and put fancy ads in print publications. Is it working? If so, why are their professionals fighting harder today to get access to new customers.

professionals are fighting harder to just "get-in"

The sales professionals know that something has changed. They know that they are working harder. They know that the prospect is more resistant than ever before to the initial request for an interview. Many of the veterans are discouraged and worn out. Building their business foundation on a selling model instead of a marketing model has taken its toll. Even those who have been successful in their careers by placing their emphasis on selling, being a great closer or knowing how to compel people to make a buying decision know that something is missing. Whatever you believe it to be, that lack of something has caused enthusiasm to wane, motivation to be lost and burnout to cause many to seek new careers.

Building a new business model for the future, based on attraction marketing and not selling, will not only be necessary for successfully reaching the customer in the near future, but it will be necessary to sustain the success and the retention of the financial professional.

We Were a Product Driven Industry

Until the early 1970s, the insurance and stock brokerage industries were product-driven, transaction oriented organizations. In 1970, the average consumer had very little if any money in stocks or mutual funds and less than $14,000 of life insurance coverage. For insurance companies, the only distinction between policy types was that insurance companies structured as mutual companies issued participating policies (called par policies) and insurance companies structured as stock companies issued nonparticipating (called nonpar policies). Participating policies paid dividends. Nonparticipating policies did not pay dividends, but they were usually twenty-five percent less expensive. As an agent, one was taught, when in competition, how to destroy the competing type of contract. Mutual companies trained their agents that stock companies paid all of their profits to their stockholders and therefore the policyholder would eventually get left out, a serious disadvantage. Stock companies trained their agents to emphasize that the IRS called dividends from mutual life insurance policies a return of premium and that was why they were tax-free. Agents were told to emphasize to the prospect, "Why would you want to pay an overcharge to your insurance company in order to get your own money back at a later date?"

Though the agents from these two different type companies were archrivals, almost everyone considered policy replacement to be unethical. Many agents prided themselves upon having been in the business for years without ever replacing a policy. They all supported their life underwriters associations and shared sales ideas willingly. Why? Because no one was doing anything different, plus "proselytizing" (stealing agents from another company) was regarded as unethical as policy replacement. Either act would incur an invitation to appear before an ethics board where one would be reprimanded and warned that another occurrence could result in expulsion from the organization.

People Were Easy to Access

There were plenty of prospects in the 1960s and '70s. Recruiting new sales representatives or agents was not difficult and, comparatively speaking, neither was getting an appointment with a prospect. People were gracious. If someone hung up on you, you were taught to call them back and apologize that somehow you must have been cut off by the telephone company. Believe it or not, you could usually continue the conversation with no one admitting any differently. A certain respect and etiquette between people was still alive and well within our society. Once you got in to see the prospect, everyone used the same sales talk, and it produced results.

Stockbrokers and insurance agents alike were all taught to sell on a one-interview approach. For the insurance industry, there were no ledger illustrations. There were only pocket rate books that contained the numbers necessary for calculating premiums, the guaranteed cash values and dividend values for providing a quote. Rate books could easily last two or three years before updating was necessary. In the early 1970s, some agents would eventually order sample ledgers, which would take five to ten days to receive from the home office. Because of the time element, multiple illustrations for prospects with ages at five-year increments, such as ages twenty-five through age fifty-five, were often ordered for creating a sales illustration book that could be shown to the prospect. The illustrations were ordered for $25,000, $50,000 and $100,000 insurance face-amounts. There was no need for any other amounts. This was a product sale and the average client was sold a $25,000 whole-life policy with guaranteed purchase options for future increases. Term insurance was expensive, really expensive after the third year, and seldom posed a problem in competition. Flexible premium contracts such as universal life had not been invented and terms such as unit cost and return on equity (ROE) were unheard of. Even Ward Cleaver ("Leave It to Beaver's" dad) was proudly portrayed as an insurance agent whom you never saw working past six p.m. and must have lived off of his renewals (that is my guess). Life was pretty good but "change" was starting to stir things up. Some agents would adjust, others would lament the good old days and fade away.

Needs-Analysis Replaces the Product Sale

Sometime around the early 1970s, a need analysis sales approach, called Capital Needs Analysis, which is attributable to Tom Wolfe, was catching on in the insurance industry. A similar planning approach was catching hold in the brokerage world. The buying public was changing. Consumers were developing an increased desire to know

The buying public was changing. Consumers were developing an increased desire to know more.

more before purchasing anything. This generation, the boomers, was better educated than any previous generation. They were watching more TV and advertisements were filling the channels. All of this contributed to a major selling change.

The 1950s ushered in the birth of modern America with its continued appetite for space exploration (NASA). The technological marvels that took us to the moon were now making an impact on American consumers with companies responding with new products and divisions established for research and development. Landing on the moon was the catalyst for a new emphasis on learning and education. People were told that they were in charge of their own destinies. The large manufacturing companies that had dominated employment in America were starting to change. They were confronting more competition and needed to respond by becoming more competitive. Ending their defined-benefit pension plans, that so many employees had considered as almost a God-given right and depended on for their retirement security, was an expense that many companies determined they could no longer continue. Inflation and then stagflation (high inflation and low unemployment) were ravaging fixed incomes and corporate profits. Housing prices were soaring, as was the cost of everything else. Mutual funds were just getting a foot hold while a recession would soon create shock waves that would see stockbrokers jumping out of windows and the adult population grasping for answers.

To add to the frustration level of many families to whom change had been so rare, the baby boomers were, on almost any subject, no longer willing to accept the traditional beliefs that their parents had always held about life in general. This new generation was starting to complete college in numbers never before seen and the beginning of the computer age had emerged. The medical courses in college were no longer the only major that had twenty-four hour open labs; the students in the computer classes now joined them. These graduating kids had more education than any previous generation. Computers had ushered in a new knowledge level with a new language that few understood, yet almost all respected. Middle age and older adults were more than willing to listen, with admiration, to the college graduate who was twenty-five to forty years younger than they, giving them advice on financial issues. Therefore, hiring fresh college grads to sell financial services to the older general public was not only encouraged, it worked (it worked far better than it does today). When prospects were called, they gave them appointments. After all, they had computer knowledge and could create financial plans. What we witnessed was an elevated trust extended to a young generation that will forever remain unique to this time in history.

The 1970s saw a technology/education gap emerge between the generations that created a

the public was tired of being sold product...

> *The agent who resisted this change was soon left behind, a fact worth remembering.*

preference for youth, instead of experience, that has never been replicated. The new college graduate was seen as intelligent and capable of providing information that was out of reach for the older generation. The older generation welcomed them in advisory capacities in spite of their youth. It is no wonder that so many young persons entered the insurance and stock brokerage industry straight out of college and succeeded. In addition, the public was tired of being sold product with no explanation. They wanted to know "WHY" and a more sophisticated needs-analysis approach was the new door opener. The agent who resisted this change was soon left behind, a fact worth remembering.

The Consultative Approach Enters the Scene

The focus on needs-analysis remained strong but made a subtle yet substantial change in the late 1970s and early 1980s. The Xerox Selling Skills course, followed by the Wilson Learning Skills program, had revolutionized the selling industry. It taught sales professionals how to conduct a consultative approach in dealing

> *the consumer…wanted less judgment extended and more listening.*

with the "new" consumer. Consumers had changed again. They no longer wanted someone to just gather objective information and return with a needs-analysis. They wanted to know that their opinions counted. More than objective facts mattered. Subjective feelings mattered as well, maybe even more. The philosophy expressed in the book, *I'm OK, You're OK* was reflective of the rise of the consumer who wanted less judgment extended and more listening. They wanted their feelings to be taken into consideration. Risk and investment tolerance questionnaires began to enter the sales process; this new consultative approach required two interviews with the prospect before being able to make a product recommendation. The one interview sales approach was fading from the scene. Quickly.

The financial planning era, along with "financial advisors" (a new identifying name), dawned in the mid-1980s. It would develop quickly with financial advisors promoting tax shelters for reducing the taxes of their clientele. The tax brackets were at the highest level the country had ever seen. These were the same ninety percent tax brackets that provided a political platform for Ronald Reagan to run for President of the United States. However, the tax shelters would eventually threaten the credibility of the whole industry as the IRS would challenge, disallow the tax deduction and charge penalties of up to fifty percent plus interest on the original deduction. In addition, most of the investments never returned even the principal investment to the investor, much less any profit. They lost it all!

Universal life was being promoted with interest rates of up to sixteen to eighteen percent with cash values projected out for

The age of skepticism was beginning to have an impact...

thirty years, forty years and sometimes more. Policy replacement of old contracts was rampant. Some companies even replaced their own client contracts to try to prevent the competition from getting to them first. Enough was enough. The industry started making attempts to regulate their own member companies but not in time to keep a major weekly national magazine from putting its well-remembered commentary on the front cover. A chimpanzee dressed like a professor, sitting on a stool, holding a piece of chalk towards a blackboard filled with numbers had a caption that read (something like), "Seems like anyone can call themselves a Financial Planner." The age of skepticism was beginning to have an impact on the financial service's industry. And it was going to get worse.

The New Client Expects a Partnership Approach

By the 1990s, the new client wanted more than just a consultant who listened during an initial approach interview and then returned with an analysis and recommendation. They wanted to be included in the decision-making process for determining solutions. They knew that there were multiple ways to approach a financial plan. The recommendation process was no longer sacred. It would become participatory. This was the advent of giving multiple-choice recommendations or partnering on the computer and allowing the prospect to feel like they were involved.

The proliferation of industry products had created parity in the eyes of the consumer. The industry had matured. The consumer believed that all companies had all products. If anyone had a competitive advantage, it would not last for long. The consumer no longer believed "Best." Best was a relative term. Product was no longer the driving force in the consumer's decision to make a purchase. The driving force was what the consumer viewed as the "package of value," which was much more than product and price.

Consumer Commonality Becomes a Core Value

In the early 1990s this era of partnership was quickly enhanced with a focus on "value commonality." The market place had once again changed and the new theory was that people would prefer to do business with those with whom they shared common values. This theory was the catalyst for encouraging sales people to target their selling activity to specific affinity groups to which they were legitimately attracted. The belief was that people who shared a common cause or who shared a common core value were more apt to grant an appointment and transact business. Salespeople were told to find their market niche, focus and work their sales plan, but something was missing.

Some organizations hired consultants to help their sales professionals learn how to market. In hindsight, most of these original marketing programs were little more than group identification programs. They lacked substance when it came to advising what to do once the financial advisor "arrived." The so-called marketing plans these consultants did promote were still based on a selling model, not a marketing model. They promoted ideas such as

...original marketing programs were little more than group identification programs.

getting the names of the group members and sending wave mailings (a staggered mailing of three letters over three weeks) with a follow-up phone call requesting an interview. By now, if one didn't look like an outsider to the group, this proved it!

The focus was still on what the sales professional could "get," a sale, versus what he could "give." The results did not deliver what was expected. Some sales professionals were all but run out of groups. They knew that they had tarnished their reputations within this group, no matter how sincerely their efforts had begun. Some sales professionals made limited sales, but this was not attraction marketing.

Companies and their sales people had great expectations for the success of these original marketing plans. They knew that the traditional methods weren't working. Retention had fallen to an all-time industry low. Sales per distribution unit were down and continued to decrease. "Getting in" was harder and every sale professional knew it. They were led to believe that marketing was the solution. The theory was right. The methods were wrong.

Attraction marketing, or better yet, Identity Branding, is about creating the future. Its purpose is to create favorable prospect attraction before the prospect has met you and well in advance of your first approach asking for an appointment. It is about building a prospect highway to a sizable prospect community that embraces you, one that can be traveled indefinitely. It is about producing a higher sense of fulfillment for the sales professional, a more assured way to build on his or her success. It is about creating a prospect preference, one that welcomes you to make the initial interview request. The goal in Identity Branding is to build a relationship, a personal connection, whose foundation is created before your first encounter – a win-win situation for everyone.

Many companies, agencies and sales associates are still trying to make a marketing plan based on a selling model. The result will be a continued disappointment until this basic mistake is corrected. Someone once said that if you are headed in the wrong direction, the last thing you want to do is to arrive there quicker. The directions and foundations of most of these plans are simply wrong.

> *Marketing, or better yet, Identity Branding, is about... building a prospect highway to a sizable prospect community that embraces you, one that can be traveled indefinitely.*

The market place has changed. Attraction marketing is not group identification; it is not about creating a clever approach letter; and success is no longer a selling game. Attraction marketing is about "getting the consumer to notice you FIRST." It is about getting the prospect attracted to you before the contact is initiated. It is about getting them to want you to contact them. The wants and needs of the consumer today may be similar to what they were ten years ago, but their ways of wanting to be approached and handled are dramatically different. If you don't

> *Marketing is about "getting the consumer to notice you FIRST."*

know the new rules, your efforts will fail. Though your plans may be called "marketing," if their foundation is flawed you will meet with discouragement. There is a better way.

IDENTITY BRANDING

Section 3

IDENTITY BRANDING

Networking,
Finding Prospects and
Capturing "Mindshare"

IDENTITY BRANDING

Accessibility to Prospects Has Decreased

A consumer marketing revolution, already underway, will continue to decrease your accessibility to prospects. Even the faces of yesterday's highly successful sales professionals may eventually fade away. To prevent this from happening to you, attraction marketing must not become just another item added to your business plan. It must become your business plan. An attraction marketing model, not a selling model, must become the driving force of your business if you are to confront this new marketing revolution successfully.

Success is no longer a game of courage contingent upon whether you can make a successful cold call. It is an attraction game. You must learn to navigate among an entirely new world of prospects or the shifting currents will eventually crush your ship. A change to the marketplace has arrived. No matter how successful you have been in the past, if you don't adjust to this change, you will suffer the unpleasant consequences that lie in wait.

The New Rules For "Getting In"

Harry Hoopis, leading general agent with Northwestern Mutual in Chicago says, "The phone has reached the level of diminishing returns. The more you use it, the less time you have to sell. It takes sixty dials per day to do what we use to do with ten dials per day. There aren't enough hours in the day to continue this trend." Michael Boylan says, in *The Power to Get In,* "…many of your desired prospects don't want to see or talk with you. If they did, you could pick up the phone and schedule all the appointments you wanted." The bottom line is that you can ignore the signs and do nothing while your market access problem worsens, and it will, or you can take a different approach and watch the market access door open wider to you while it closes further to the competition that remains unenlightened.

To win in this new environment, you will need to successfully accomplish two things. First, you must find a specific market(s) segment focus that possesses two criteria. It must be suitable and it must emotionally pull your interest. Secondly you must construct an arrival action plan so that when you get market active you can become identified by the prospect as distinctively different from the competition.

> *...you will need to successfully accomplish two things...find a specific market(s) segment focus...and construct an arrival action plan*

What Market Will You Target?

The first element that must be addressed is what market you will target. Dr. Thomas Stanley, in his book *Networking With The Affluent,* says, "Too few sales professionals target effectively." Most sales professionals and companies think they are targeting because they can give a generic targeting description, such as small business owners, for their focus. That description is simply too general! If the truth were known, most sales professionals are still contacting any referral they are given (especially by their largest clients) as long as they feel they can get a "respectable size check," which they proudly acknowledge as larger than that of most of their less experienced peers. This is hardly the idea of

> *Most sales professionals and companies think they are targeting because they can give a generic targeting description, such as small business owners, for their focus. That description is simply too general!*

marketing. Their efforts are more similar to a continual hunting and killing expedition. Their resilience may be commendable, but this type of focus eventually wears out even the most committed.

Identifying an affinity group, such as homebuilders or occupational therapists that you may want to target is important, but simply identifying a group is not marketing. It is only the initial step in positioning. It is comparable to a lumberjack standing at night between the city lights and the forest in an initial attempt to decide which direction to head in the morning. His initial conclusion should give him a good sense of direction as to which way he should go to get to his group of trees, but nothing more.

What Is an Effective Market Segment?

Professional salespersons do not survive when they continue to view the entire world as their market. However, unless their product line is user specific to a very narrow group of consumers, neither do they normally focus entirely on only one segment of individuals. Most sales professionals will have one to three, three usually being the maximum, well-defined and identifiable groups that they consider their primary market and to which they focus their attention. After you have thought through who in your personal sphere (i.e., friends, acquaintances, fellow church members, civic club associates) should be included in your market and your strategy to Identity Brand your reputation, you will need to determine where your prospect highway to a larger prospect community needs to be constructed. This will vary from one individual to another and from one geographical area to another. You may find welcomed access in one city and resistance in another. Once you have decided on the market segment(s) that you want to concentrate on, your efforts should now be focused on individualizing your market by identifying a significant number of prospect names for inclusion into your *Prospect Fishbowl™*.

There should be two primary components present in selecting a market segment before putting a great effort into individualizing your market by attaining specific prospect names and then beginning the process to Identity Brand your reputation. The first component should be consideration of size. Considering that it will take a dedication of effort to become distinctly positioned as the brand of choice, you will want to be assured that your efforts are impacting an adequate number of prospects necessary to meet your goals. It will take as much effort to influence a group of fifty people as it would a group of five hundred. Considering that you are limited by the number of hours for this task, if you know that you will need to influence a thousand prospects over the next few years, don't get involved with a group of fewer than two hundred people.

The number two component for selecting an appropriate market segment is that the sales professional must have an affinity for the segment, a social connection or share a belief commonality to it. If you don't like the people or the cause, don't attempt to build a prospect highway to the group. You will never be able to identify or communicate well to it. Don't get attracted solely by prestige or net worth. Yes, they need to be able to afford whatever you are offering; however, you must find a group that you share a commonality with and one that you genuinely like, one that creates an emotional pull. Simply stated, find a kindred spirit.

Here is a market segment definition for consideration in focusing your thoughts:

A market should be an identifiable segment of people who knowingly share a significant commonality, which may be based on:

• *Occupation*

• *A deep dedication to a special interest (usually hobbies, recreation or clubs)*

• *A significant involvement with a community or a civic organization*

• *An organized, deeply shared social cause*

• *A life-defining religious following*

• *A cohesive ethnic group who regularly network and communicate with each other.*

When I find a professional salesperson who is attempting to market to a defined market segment, who has a well thought through attraction plan but is struggling with attaining results, I normally find that the market definition has been compromised or their personal commonality (emotional pull) to the segment is weak, possibly nonexistent. We will discuss that further in the next few pages.

Individualize Your Market

Choosing an appropriate market segment is the beginning step in

IDENTITY BRANDING

> *...you must "individualize" the future customer [prospect] not as a group but as a person.*

deciding toward whom to direct your efforts. However, as Lynn Upshaw says, in *Building Brand Identity,* "Smart brand marketers rethink who their targets are by acknowledging that they are not targets at all, but individual human beings." He believes that you must "individualize" the future customer [prospect] not as a group but as a person. You must know by name those whom you want to influence, those from whom you want to capture "mindshare" over the next months and years. Then you must increase their familiarization with you.

Ford Harding, in his book *Creating Rainmakers,* defines rainmakers as those professionals who have an uncanny ability to create leads and sales results that are far superior to the other professionals in their firms. As individuals, the main element of their success is expressed as, "The rainmakers never lost track of a client or prospective client or other important contact. Once they develop a relationship with someone, they never let go." He further states, "...rainmakers build big networks...and...strive to stay in front of their network

> *These super achievers built a foundational Prospect Fishbowl of at least 1,000 prospects...*

members' minds." Because of this constant one-to-one familiarization, these people eventually become clients; the sales professional knows exactly whom to cultivate, whom to direct their Identity Branding efforts to, whom to send e-newsletters to, whom to consistently invite to events. These super achievers built a foundational *Prospect Fishbowl* of at least 1,000 prospects and then focused their attention to adding, nurturing, and learning to migrate (versus prospect) among the individuals in a way that the individuals appreciated. Their primary focus changes from prospecting to maintaining continual familiarization (migrating within their *Prospect Fishbowl™*) by providing value in order to capture "mindshare," which in turn creates prospect attraction.

A thought-provoking commentary on rainmakers was written in the January 10, 2000 edition of Forbes magazine. The article, authored by Robert Lenzner and Ashlea Ebeling, was titled "A Wealth of Names-David Rockefeller Sr. is the Ultimate Rainmaker." The article begins, "You can measure David Rockefeller Sr.'s wealth and power by taking a look at his stock portfolio, his real estate holdings or his art collection. Or you can take an elevator to the 56th floor of Rockefeller Center in New York and look for an alcove that encloses a massive Ferris wheel of a Rolodex. This 4-foot-by-5-foot contraption is the fulcrum of Rockefeller's globe-trotting life at the age of 84." The Rolodex contains 150,000 names. Is it any wonder why David Rockefeller Sr. is perhaps the number-one money raiser for philanthropic causes in the world today, much less why he was and still is a world tycoon of a businessperson? The article calls his Rolodex, "a working man's toolbox" and finishes with "That Rolodex is worth a fortune...but you can't put a value on it."

> *The Rolodex contains 150,000 names.*
>
> *"That Rolodex is worth a fortune...but you can't put a value on it."*

As you consider your efforts in individualizing your prospect market, remember the lesson from David Rockefeller Sr. He never could have attained the success in his endeavors without knowing and inserting his prospects by name, one-by-one, into his database. A general description of a market segment would never have supported Rockefeller's accomplishments, and neither will it for you. You don't need 150,000 names to meet your goals, but you will need more than your closest one hundred friends, your list of two hundred clients or the remaining thirty-five referrals that you have stacked on your desk to call on.

What to Do Once You Get Market Active

Once you identify the market segment(s) that you believe you want to focus your efforts towards, you would be ill-advised to start your attraction marketing efforts by sending multiple sales solicitation letters (often called wave-mails) to the members and then calling for an appointment. You would have more failure than success. Why? Because this technique will verify to the membership that you are an "outsider." Why would you need to send a solicitation letter to a colleague if you were an "insider" who had the group's respect? You have ruined the perception that you have the group's deep concerns as part of your interest. Their perception will be that your interest in regard to their cause is not genuine, has no real emotional connection and neither is it a life-long commitment. The perception is that you are here "to get" and not "to give." Your multiple letter-mailing programs within a cohesive market segment will either fail miserably or after it has resulted in some minor successes you will be well aware that you have worn out your welcome and your future success in this group will be limited. You will now need to find a new group and start the process all over again. So much for solicitation letters being the solution to solving your life-long prospecting and market access problems. This is an unfortunate story that has been repeated far too many times within our industry.

The sales professional who joins a group and after numerous years has developed a limited number of clients within the group also has a brand personality problem. Most likely, they still feel awkward, almost embarrassed, to request an interview with another group member in hopes of beginning a business relationship. Just ask a sales professional. In an environment where they can safely talk, they will verify this. The issue is not whether they are missing opportunities in front of their noses; the issue is why has it been so difficult to transition prospects into clients. They know that they have developed no personal business preference although they may have been involved with this group for years. They have never had an adequate prospect attraction plan that was structured to direct their "what to do" efforts once they arrived.

We have an attraction marketing problem and an arrival problem within this industry. In a mature industry built on a selling model and not an attraction-marketing model, once the general consumer

We have a marketing problem and an arrival problem within this industry.

believed that they were adequately acquainted with the product, what else could you expect to develop but a market access problem? The novelty of the product or service would no longer suffice for getting in the door.

The financial industry, as a whole, has placed almost their entire emphasis on getting new associates off to a fast selling start rather than helping them identify a significant foundational prospect market and delivering their professional business reputation to it. Having the advisor begin their career with contacting their one hundred or two hundred personal friends is not a significant foundational market. Without significant market prospects, accompanied by a strategy for delivering one's personal business reputation to them, the sale professional's motivation will even-

tually fade, as well as their chances of long-term success. It is no wonder why most advisors eventually give up. They were taught how to sell, but not how to deliver themselves to a market audience.

The challenge is to learn how to deliver YOU to your audience.

The psychological elements necessary for an individual to sustain motivation are based on behavior requested and the consequences incurred. If positive consequences are not incurred in adequate numbers as to the behavior being requested, the individual will eventually curtail the activity, if not stop entirely. When the only positive consequence of a fast-start selling endeavor is an immediate "sale," you will more than likely have inadequate successes to sustain most people's motivation. On the other hand, if the fast-start behavior were redefined to accumulating prospect names and employing a strategy for delivering impressions to a defined prospect community, numerous activities on a daily basis could be defined as success and motivation would be sustained until the market were receptive to the professional's contact. Until the industry starts emphasizing building a substantial individualized prospect foundation, before focusing their emphasis on getting the sales associate off to a fast (selling) start, we will continue to see eroding retention. We will also continue to find senior agents who after ten, fifteen, or twenty years, have still not delivered themselves as unique to their local market, and still struggle with prospect access.

Address the prospect attraction issue or your problems will get worse.

It is no wonder that insurance agents and financial advisors are leaving their parent companies and agencies to become affiliated with banks or even competing organizations that have a perceived "higher profile." The perception is that these organizations have a greater client "mindshare" and that it is easier to get in front of the prospect. The manager's response has been, "But you're losing ownership of your block of business! Look at all you are giving up." The agents' and financial advisors' response, though normally not verbalized, has been, "No... You don't understand. Look at all I am gaining." It is not the competition that is affecting you. The marketing revolution is affecting you! If you don't address the prospect attraction issue, your problems will get worse.

Call Reluctance Can Increase

If the sale professionals involved in specific market segments were successful in Identity Branding themselves as the "mark of excellence" within their field, I believe that call reluctance would eventually be replaced with call enthusiasm. They would eventually sense that they own the market because of the value they have given. However, until that happens, they will be reluctant to initiate a selling contact while not really knowing how the group perceives them, as an insider or an outsider. To compound the problem, after a while they will have established friends within the group. If they don't know how their contact for business will be received, they won't initiate a call. It is much harder on the sales professional to be turned down by a friend than it is by a stranger. Although they may not have achieved business "mindshare," they have made friends. Their friendship, with the development of no market preference, no "mindshare," no strategy for building prospect attraction, will emotionally stop their well-planned intentions to call on these people whom they originally targeted.

If networking provides so much, why is it that networking is such an anomaly to so many sales professionals and managers? It is one of the most critical items for effective marketing and it is critical to the success of most sales professionals. However, it is seldom done. My conclusion is that networking is one of the most misunderstood items within all selling professions. Not only is it done poorly, the purpose is usually improperly defined. Those two elements alone render it practically impossible to attain great results. So let's start by defining the purpose of networking and then defining how to do it.

The Purpose of Networking

Initially, networking's purpose is to meet significant groups of potential prospects with the intention of being able to "give," not "get." In today's age of consumer skepticism, if your intention is to meet people so that you can "get" instead of "give," your success will be limited. People prefer to buy from people whom they perceive as popular, someone with

if your intention is to... "get" instead of "give," your success will be limited.

a distinct reputation, someone who is a little bit famous. You cannot become popular by meeting someone and then immediately telling them about yourself while attempting to get what you want instead of providing what they want. Effective networking begins by asking about them, determining how you can help in their personal or business objectives. If done properly, networking can become your number-one way to accumulate prospect names for your *Prospect Fishbowl*, persons you will then want to influence and cultivate with value information delivered uniquely over time. Eventually, networking's primary purpose will change from building an abundance of qualified prospect names to deepening the "mindshare" of the identified prospects. However, you will always be on the alert to find new prospects to replace your less desirable ones as your *Prospect Fishbowl* evolves through your success and your increasing skill level.

Research among the leading sales professionals indicates that your *Prospect Fishbowl* should have a minimum of 1,000 names. The nationally known financial service company, Edward Jones Investments, best illustrates the results that this can incur. Edward Jones Investments has one of the highest retention ratios for sales professionals in the industry, over eighty-five percent for first-year sales associates and over seventy percent for fifth-year sales associates. Compare that to an industry retention ratio of between eleven to fifteen percent! It is reported that their average income for fifth-year sales professionals exceeds $150,000. Because they expect an associate to build an inventory of approximately 1,500 prospects and to have personally met all of them within their first three to six months, is it any wonder why their retention and success ratios are so high?

The Edward Jones new representative's main focus for four months is to meet twenty-five prospects per day, Monday through Saturday, with an objective to initiate a relationship rather than an immediate sale. That initial meeting provides the representative with the prospect's permission to begin the process of familiarization through future educational mailings and invitations to investment events. Representatives build an initial prospect foundation to which they can focus their efforts to consistently familiarize themselves to individuals, not just to a generic target market. These initial daily contacts result in providing frequent positive feedback, which creates emotional building blocks that sustains the representative's motivation and confidence.

Success is not defined by, nor dependent on making a sale – not for the first four months. The representative's motivation is sustained from the daily positive prospect contacts and from knowing that their present efforts are cultivating the fields of their future success. The Edward Jones Company helps lay solid marketing foundations for their sales associates and they don't veer from their structure. If you want to do it another way, find another firm. It won't be Edward Jones.

The Edward Jones Investment Company, along with Wal-Mart and Southwest Airlines, is currently a curriculum case study in the Harvard School of Business because of their high level of success with their customers and their sales organization. One Harvard professor is said to frequently comment that the Edward Jones Company appears to have been designed by the customer. I am sure that the Edward Jones Company focus, on providing consistent value information to identified individual prospects, makes the prospects and clients feel that these Edward Jones representatives are focused on giving first and getting second, the basis for a business that attracts customers.

To be a successful networker your actions must convey that your networking activities are about the prospect and not for telling about yourself. Marketing and networking require consistency, no different than achieving a health-fitness goal. It takes patience and perseverance. Most agents give up on marketing efforts way too prematurely, and with the companies emphasis on fast sales results, it's almost impossible to refocus them back on

> *Marketing is…about providing value, eventually capturing "mindshare"*

marketing and on developing a prospect foundation before a career crisis sets in. Getting a sale is certainly part of what a selling profession is all about, but it is initially the wrong focus for the agents first few months and the low industry retention ratio proves it. Attraction marketing is not about meeting people to see what you can get from them within the shortest possible time frame. It is about providing value, eventually capturing "mindshare" and creating consumer preference, which then provides market access to people wanting to see you.

How to Begin Networking

So, how do you get started? If I were an experienced sale professional, I would start with identifying my most successful clients, whom I would clone numerous times, if I could. If I were a new associate, I would start by identifying friends and acquaintances whom I would like to have as clients and if I could replicate them a hundred times over, I would. I would identify three of my best, make an appointment, tell them how highly I think of them and explain my purpose. I would tell them that I am specializing my "practice" by narrowing my market focus to three affinity groups within which I want to concentrate the majority of my work. I would explain that I was hoping they might assist me in accomplishing that goal. Ask them what occupational associations they belong to and start there. It is fine if you need to use a questionnaire of sorts (refer to available resources in the back of the book), but make sure that they realize that you are asking questions to determine what you can give and not what you can get.

Be practical. If you don't want to work with schoolteachers, don't initiate a marketing conversation with one. Start with individuals whom you believe represent an industry that has both sufficient quantity and financial promise. Don't get discouraged if, as you get more information, you find that your group has limited potential. Choosing a market segment to target is not an exact science. Sometimes you will be fooled. Parker Palmer, author of Let Your Life Speak, says that in life as in any experiment, "negative results are at least as important as successes." Don't let a false start discourage you. You will learn a lot even from a failure should you experience one. Just expect that one out of three times your initiative to get involved with a market segment group will be wrong, so find another group and try again. Trust that your perseverance will be rewarded.

Some groups you may want to consider as potential market segments are homebuilders, general contractors, home remodelers, building material supply associations, HVAC contractors, plumbers, electricians, pest control associations, automobile dealer associations, printers, human resource associations, snack food vendors, forest farmers, lumber companies, dairy farmers, poultry farmers and suppliers, restaurant associations and restaurant suppliers, furniture manufacturers, textile manufacturers, United Arts Council, The National Association of Christians and Jews, and even coaches of local youth soccer, baseball and basketball teams. The list can go on forever! For your local associations, look in the Association's Yellow Book at your local library. It will list them all and will also provide a lot of information to help you evaluate your initial choices.

Write down your ideas for specific market segments that provide a good focus and how you can obtain names for your *Prospect Fishbowl.*

Brand Positioning and Personality Are Imperative

The more specialized and distinct you can appear, the more attractive you become to your prospects. Lynn Upshaw, in *Building Brand Identity,* says, "simply building a brand identity fortress [name recognition] is not enough." You must create personal brand personality to successfully attract the consumer. In other words, name recognition only does not create prospect attraction, brand positioning or brand personality, all of which are necessary to create consumer attraction. Upshaw furthers this thought by saying, "When the strategic personality and positioning have been successfully blended, the result is a brand essence that is hard for prospects to ignore." Name only

> *Service keeps clients. It doesn't attract new prospects. ...creating a **local** Identity Brand attracts new prospects.*

does not drive the consumer to purchase your product or to want to meet with you. Neither will striving to perform your job better than the competition nor providing better service, though both are admirable goals. Service keeps clients. It doesn't attract new prospects. Building a personal, differentiated, local Identity Brand attracts new prospects.

Without the brand components of positioning and personality, the argument that branding has occurred, particularly in a financial services industry, is hardly supportable unless the definition of branding is narrowed to being the company with the highest level of name recognition. That definition, however, is inappropriate. Branding is about creating consumer attraction. Without that element, highly recognizable names such as Yugo and Edsel would be thriving brand products with consumer appeal. Obviously, they are not and neither is the sales professional who believes he or she is well positioned because they represent the insurance company or brokerage firm with the highest name recognition. Unless the representative creates personal brand positioning and brand personality locally, increasing the degree of your company's national name recognition will provide little impact on your ability "to get in." The focus must turn to getting YOU to become distinctively different and unique. As your identity distinction increases locally, so does your initial consumer attraction. The degree of your local Identity Brand is what measures the level of your attractiveness to the consumer.

> *...increasing the degree of your company's national name recognition will provide little impact on your ability "to get in."*
>
> *The degree of your local Identity Brand is what measures the level of your attractiveness...*

How to Become Meaningfully Involved

The best networkers become involved with the group, give noticeable value, demonstrate appreciation for the organization and become uniquely visible. For instance, they may approach the board of directors of the city's recreational soccer league and offer to sponsor an appreciation night for the coaches, their market segment, by buying out an entire evening of a small local theater production and honoring them (the cost to do this is usually around $1,200). Consider cosponsoring this appreciation event with a wine merchant and include a free wine tasting during a thirty-minute intermission. The wine merchant will provide the wine for free and would probably share the cost of the theater tickets. Obviously, you both would receive a lot of recognition for doing this and these people have now entered your *Prospect Fishbowl* for further familiarization over time.

Think about becoming involved with an organization and

volunteering to help in fund-raising for their cause. For instance, you may have a real compassion for helping less financially fortunate people obtain home ownership and Habitat for Humanity would be a cause that could emotionally capture your interest. With your talent in sales, offer to help with corporate giving instead of, or in addition to, pounding nails. Become their number-one fundraiser! Not only will you feel good but also the group, as well as the business people from whom you solicit charitable contributions, will esteem you. There is no more honorable person than the person who does something to help someone else. Think of this same example with Hospice, The Childhood Leukemia Foundation or even your local college or university's athletic scholarship program. You didn't have to be graduated from there to recognize the value that a strong university adds to the quality of life in your town, so get involved and help raise money. If you become the best fundraiser, you will see the payoff in numerous ways. Be patient and consistent and save all of your contact names in your *Prospect Fishbowl*. You will continue to build a familiarization with these same prospects by continuing to provide valuable information over time.

Giving is the essence of high-performance networking. The Bible, says, "It is more blessed to give than to receive." If you *quit figuring out how to send a catchy solicitation letter...* want to attract favorable attention from your prospects, quit figuring out how to send a catchy solicitation letter (much less a multiple letter attack on colored paper) and start giving value to a group or organization that you care about. Build respect from within the group and you will get noticed, appreciated and eventually wealthy.

Build A Distinct and Unique Image

In order to become an effective networker you must learn how to develop "mindshare" within your individualized *Prospect Fishbowl.* Dan Kennedy, author of *The Ultimate Marketing Plan,* says, "Find your most promotable competitive edge, turn it into a powerful marketing message and deliver it to the right prospects." Dan is not referring to a general and nonindividualized target market. Neither is he referring to product features and benefits as your competitive edge. He is referring to individualizing your target market and promoting your personal distinction and uniqueness relative to the competition.

Most financial sales professionals think of print advertising when the word promotion is used. Don't! You must be more in the mind of the prospect than just a quality, knowledgeable professional who represents quality products and services, which is all that print advertising can convey. Those benefits alone are no longer adequate and neither does the prospect see them as distinctive. Furthermore, most sales professionals and companies view the world through product knowledge versus marketing knowledge. They believe that providing more advanced training for creating superior knowledge in product and service, relative to the competition, will increase prospect attraction. This is a faulty diagnosis of a marketing problem and an inaccurate conclusion. The focus should be to make YOU, a little bit famous, not your company.

Image is built from being distinct and unique through providing experiences...

Here is how you want to start. In order to begin creating a personal and distinctive business image you must first begin building an individualized *Prospect Fishbowl.* Choose a market segment(s), remember, no more than three and each one being sufficient in size (200+). If this group has a membership, make sure that you join once you are satisfied that the group is cohesive, large enough and can financially support your business focus. You will never be considered a colleague to a "membership group" unless you are a member. As part of your market segment(s), you may select a charitable organization where you can become highly recognized for your efforts in fundraising. Dr. Thomas Stanley, in *Networking With the Affluent,* says, "…affluent prospects see you at your best when you are helping others you volunteer for." So get involved. Get noticed. Be the best at the job and don't ever lose a name that you have encountered. Always build and continue to add to your *Prospect Fishbowl.*

What About Sending a Newsletter?

Don't confuse quarterly newsletters, magazines or annual reports with attraction marketing. They deliver an impact that is equal to a client seeing a billboard. They are very rarely read but serve as validation that you are still around. However, sending a newsletter to a prospect is a different issue. Don't assume that these make a favorable impact on your prospects. They don't! Newsletters are not unique. Neither do they profile YOU. They are not helpful in attracting the prospect who is waiting to see your personal distinction within the market. Remember, it is YOU that needs to be created as distinct and unique, not your company.

You do need to decide how to maintain a consistent familiarization to the individual prospect within your market, but newsletters are not the answer. We have commented frequently in this book that just because you go to the local homebuilder's association each month, the Rotary meeting every week or even become the best fund-raiser for Habitat for Humanity, doesn't mean you have captured preference in regard to your business. The author Dr. Thomas Stanley, says, "…the very best sellers and marketers offer clients much more than a core and often mundane product." There is nothing more mundane than a newsletter. What is it that you offer to capture "mindshare?" Keep reading. The answers are still coming.

Creating Low Cost Unique Events and Finding Potential Market Allies

To become a personal Identity Brand within a specific prospect market segment, your familiarization plan must favorably differentiate you from the competition. A perception of being unique and distinct must permeate your reputation. Conducting no less than two annual events per year to which you invite your *Prospect Fishbowl* will create a competitive advantage and start you well on your way to becoming the most recognizable and distinct professional within your market. Regis McKenna, author of *Real Time*, says, "Brand is more than a name. Brand is an

> *Regis McKenna, author of Real Time, says, "Brand is more than a name. Brand is an active experience."*

active experience." The more creative you can be, the more distinctive your Identity Brand becomes. Even those who don't attend will take notice of the invitation and the uniqueness. Either way, the perception of appearing unique to the prospect has been accomplished. You are starting to build a local quality perception whose distinctiveness will eventually become your brand.

To appear unique, to reduce cost and to attract new prospects to your events, consider allying yourself with someone who desires the same type of exposure to similar types of prospects. For instance, invite a psychologist to conduct a yearly event on "How to Help Students With Learning Disabilities Choose a College and Complete Their Degrees." You can send a letter inviting any parent of school age children to attend. The presentation is shared as well as the cost, which should be minimal if the event is held in a library, college, etc. Another example is to become known for conducting an annual event at the beginning of every new year such as, "The Best Investments and Best All-Inclusive Vacations For the New Year – An Evening of Fun." Not only could a local travel agency share the cost but you could also ask a new catering company to participate by providing hors d'oeuvres at cost. Invite them both to contribute their client lists for the mailing. This is a great promotion for you and it benefits the travel and catering companies as well. Your prospects are the same prospects they want to influence.

Now that your creative mind is working, how about conducting a bi-annual investment event, "A Taste of Wine for the Autumn Times – An Evening of Wine Tasting and Investment Tips"? Guess who provides the wine FOR FREE? The wine merchant! Just ask. Follow-up with a spring theme so that you are conducting two consistent events per year. Consistency creates local market validation, regarding your claim of business uniqueness. It

Invite your best forty clients to an annual client appreciation night called, "Croquet and Chardonnay–Please Wear Your English Whites for an Evening of Merriment."

proves that you are distinct. Print the dates of your two yearly investment events on the back of your business card, or on a separate card, and accentuate your local distinction, as compared to the competition.

Invite your best forty clients to an annual client appreciation night called,"Croquet and Chardonnay - Please Wear Your English Whites for an Evening of Merriment." Mention in the invitation that this is a "Friends Bringing Friends" event. Accentuate that aspect and your *Prospect Fishbowl* will be the recipient of numerous new prospects whom will be impressed with your uniqueness relative to the competition.

If you're a financial advisor attempting to build your brand presence, while adding qualified prospect names to your *Prospect Fishbowl,* here is a unique idea, but only if the commonality is genuine. Get a local theater to allow you to purchase an entire mid-morning showing (approximately $300-$500) of an appropriate movie for children such as The Prince of Egypt. Align yourself with the leading Christian bookstore in your area. Promote the event with a mailer, which you produce, and with additional flyers to be handed out at the bookstore's cash register. Both should include the message that you and the bookseller both appreciate the customer's patronage of the bookstore. The free children's tickets are available at the bookstore for clients and customers who come into the store to register. Plan for a three-hour event and contact the local YMCA or a church junior high youth group about providing teenage chaperones (usually free or for a very small donation). Give away helium balloons; hold drawings for children's prizes, a twenty-five dollar gift certificate from the bookstore and four tickets to the theater, which will be donated. Use the forms the parents fill out to register their children for the free movie as the entry forms for the drawings. Make sure that the form includes the parent's name, address, phone number and email address. Remember, these new people go into your *Prospect Fishbowl* for further familiarization over time.

The next few pages contain a few examples of invitations inviting prospects and clients to unique events that demonstrate aligning yourself with market allies.

In Appreciation For Your Business

A Child's Morning Out

Agape Christian Bookstore and (name) invites your children
to enjoy a free exclusive showing of *The Prince of Egypt*.
It's our way of saying THANKS for your patronage!

Saturday, January 22, 2000
9:00am - 12:00 noon
The Local Theatre
777 North Point Parkway
Greensboro, NC

The fun begins with doughnuts & juice, a balloon magician
and other special entertainment for the kids before
the featured movie and popcorn. While the kids
enjoy their morning out and a movie, you can
enjoy your morning out. Call and register
at Agape Christian Bookstore at
(phone #). Please thank our
co-sponsor and friend
(name again)

ADMIT ONE

ADMIT ONE

Invitation design © Glad Tidings, Inc., Dallas 75229 (88437)

Viva Italia!
AN ANNUAL CLIENT APPRECIATION NIGHT
Friends Bringing Friends

Agent X and High Trust Insurance Company cordially invite you to enjoy an unforgettable evening at our Annual Client Appreciation Italian Festival. Spend an evening with other clients, plus bring your friends, and indulge yourself with fabulous Italian food along with an Italian wine tasting and dancing. Enjoy an intriguing presentation during dinner on *Italy – How to go and what to see*, presented by (travel group) and a 12-minute presentation on *12-Month Economic Forecast and Investment Predictions*. Now, bring out the band... Let's dance the evening away! Don't miss this event!

Saturday, January 15, 2005
7:00 pm – 11:00 pm
Country Club, City

Reservations are needed. Space is limited so *RSVP* early by contacting (name) at 336-303-7316.
Invitation design © Four Seasons Publishing, Inc. Portland, ME (No. I-211)

Recreating Traditional Events to Attract More Attendees

The birth of any brand is always initiated with an experience that impacts the prospect. The establishment of brand preference, within the consumers mind, is the culmination of repeated and multiple experiences and consistent familiarization. There is a tremendous benefit in consistently conducting periodic traditional events, such as bringing in mutual fund managers in order to continually impact your individualized market segment(s). You can increase attendance, as well as your distinctiveness, by stamping them with your personal touch by being creative in naming these events.

Instead of simply inviting prospects and clients to quarterly investment seminars, briefs or workshops, all of which have been overdone, invite them to "events" and give them more intriguing titles such as, "Predictions Revealed for Attaining 'Home Run' Investment Returns Over the Next Five Years." Doesn't that title sound more interesting than "Opportunities in Value Investing"? How about, "The Newest Secrets for Maximizing Returns [including your 401(k) account], Minimizing Risk and 'Smashing Those Taxes' " or "Securing Large Profits While Avoiding Deep Losses! The Stock Market Will Make a Correction." These titles are much more appealing, distinctive and memorable than, "Stock Market Trends and Opportunities" or "Tax Smart Investing." Try to use words that elicit emotion, attract curiosity and imply that you may have information that your prospects and clients would like to have; words such as, "secrets," "predictions," "avoid," or "revealing" are intriguing and difficult words to ignore. Here is one final example: "The 'Newest' Investment Secrets that You Must Know for Attaining Superior Returns." Creative titles will draw more attraction and help in creating your Identity Brand of being distinct, unique and differentiated relative to the competition.

Usually the broker dealer will assume most of the cost for these events. You just need to get the attendees there. If you have your *Prospect Fishbowl* built, that will be easy. Imagine the impact on your prospects as they continually get invited to pre-set bi-annual unique events and receive consistent intellectual communications from you. Remember, any of these events can be promoted as "Friends Bringing Friends." Set your strategy now to do two events per year and begin proclaiming that these are part of your market differentiation, as compared to the competition.

Write down some ideas for your consistent events that would help Identity Brand your distinction within your market segment.

Get Published in a Trade Journal or Newsletter

What else can you do? How about writing an article for publication in your group association's newsletter or trade journal? Just call the publications editors and ask. They will treat you like a gift from heaven. The article could be on risk management, investing or tax reduction strategies, but it could also be something creative such as "Why The New Marketing Revolution Will Change Your Company's Marketing Strategy" or "What the 21st Century Consumer Wants...It's More Than Your Core Product or Service." You might create an article on "Effective Selling Methods to Increase Sales" by applying your selling system to their type of product or service. Topics that offer clients information to enhance their income are appreciated far more than self-promotion. Whatever your topic, the tagline at the end of the article always identifies you to the audience as the contributing author. Be sure that you make reprints. Give them generously to the people in your *Prospect Fishbowl* that you want to influence. Send one to a prospect whom you want to get an appointment with and watch the door open when you call for the request. Keep a stack of reprints for future use. Getting published in their trade journal or local newsletter is a great way to validate your expertise to your prospect and to differentiate you from the competition. However, don't assume that everyone saw or will remember your article. Feel free to give them a little help. Promote your accomplishment.

List opportunities and topic ideas for writing an article.

Don't Golf in a Sponsored Golf Tournament

Many organizations sponsor yearly golf tournaments such as the Homebuilders Association, the Country Club's Member-Guest tournament, the Chamber of Commerce, The Merchant's Association, American Heart and Lung Association, Cancer Association, or the Manufacturers Association. Even most religious denominations sponsor a summer tournament for their members.

Do NOT sign up to play golf with a foursome!

Other companies hold yearly golf tournaments to promote good will, such as Enterprise Rental Car who extends invitations to their corporate clients to participate. If you really love golf, call every golf club, private or public, and ask who is holding a tournament and the cost of sponsoring a hole, usually one-hundred to two-hundred dollars max. They will enthusiastically give you the information. Now...DON'T GOLF IN THE TOURNAMENT! Ask to sponsor the watering hole. That's the hole that supplies free beer and soft drinks to the golfers. Tell them that you will take a digital picture of each foursome, conduct a longest drive marshmallow contest, and send an e-photo album to each golfer, thanking them for participating. You can also announce the winners and how much money was raised for "the cause" due to their participation. Next year, you can volunteer to send e-invitations to the participants or provide the organization with the email addresses. Make sure that you bring a lawn chair and a yellow legal pad (or index cards). That's for the golfers to write their name and email address. If you use pre-printed cards, you can ask for their employer, birth date, financial areas of interest, and any other information that you want.

Want to be exceptionally memorable? Tell the golfers that your hole is a "win-a-car" hole, without the hole-in-one requirement – just closest to the pin will win (or longest marshmallow drive will win). If you do the marshmallow drive, have 3 marshmallows for each golfer. They will all be laughing and asking for multiple marshmallows since this is such a novelty. As far as the car goes, they will all tell you that you are lying, but have fun and kid with them that it is absolutely true. Have a matchbox car hidden your pocket. They only cost eighty-nine cents each. After they all hit their golf ball, pull out the matchbox car and present it to the golfer who won. Take another picture of the golfer (or foursome) with the matchbox car in hand. They will love it! You will be remembered at the end for the day as the most fun hole to have visited. The matchbox car will become an icon during the tournament. Look distinct. Be different! And remember that exceptional difference is what pays off the most!

If appropriate, bring along a quantity of cigars, both tobacco and bubble gum so that no one feels left out. Get the one-dollar golf specials. Any cigar shop can help you out. Many will give you cigars for free if they can stand at the hole with you and promote their tobacco shop.

Here is the type of dialogue that should occur in an initial contact with the golf course contact:

(Name of person), as a part of my annual plans for contributing back to groups in which I do a lot of business, I try to sponsor a golf tournament each year in order to see old friends and clients, as well as meet new people in an atmosphere where everyone is having fun. When I sponsor a golf hole, I always take pictures of each foursome and then send each person a photo of the tournament along with final results – both of the scoring, the winning golfers and the amount money raised for the organization. I also get the e-mail addresses so we can send the photo album to each participant – plus I will provide a copy of the e-mail database to your organization so you can invite the players back next year – or I can do it for you. We find that taking pictures always works best at the watering hole, where the foursomes seem to get very social. If play gets backed up, we

usually have a marshmallow-driving contest (longest drive) at our hole and give out prizes to the winner. Teeing of marshmallows is always a smile inducing moment. In other words, we try to make our hole a really memorable event. Can you tell me if the watering hole would be a possibility?

When the golf tournament is over, send the e-photo album out to each participant within three days. Follow up with sending an e-Financial Storyboard, accentuating your professional business image in another five days. You will get a lot of favorable responses and leads.

Participating in a golf tournament, in this manner, is unique and you will get many favorable comments. The fund-raising committee will think you are a genius. You can easily get a roster of foursomes in the order that they will arrive at your hole. You will know their names except for the last-minute substitutions and you can verify all names, company affiliations and addresses as you take their picture. Except for your financial service competitor, who came past your hole with the three clients that he invited to play, put everyone else into your *Prospect Fishbowl*. These people will eventually be easy to request appointments with.

Cigar Aficionados

You may want to make a special note of the serious cigar smokers when sponsoring your golf tournament. In the future, when you organize a cigar-dinner event, co-sponsored with a cigar store (they will supply free cigars), a wine merchant (free wine)and a new caterer (food at cost and split three ways), these are great people to include on the invitation list. The format for this event opens with thirty minutes of hors d'oeuvres. Invite the guests to be seated at rectangular tables arranged at forty-five degree angles so that everyone can see the front of the room (don't use round tables). Begin the evening with a fifteen-minute presentation introducing the first cigar. Follow this with a ten-minute presentation introducing the first wine and then complete this first segment with a ten to twelve-minute presentation on investment strategies. Invite a mutual fund manager to be present and they will normally pay for all or part of the food cost. Break for a forty-five minute pasta bar extravaganza. Reconvene for the second segment in which the order of presentations is reversed: investments (twelve minutes), wine (ten minutes) and a final cigar presentation (fifteen minutes). Place evaluation forms at the tables during the pasta course for collection at the end. Announce that a drawing for a few bottles of wine, another one for six fine cigars and a final one for a free copy of a best selling business or financial book such as The Millionaire Next Door, by Dr. Thomas Stanley will be conducted at the end of the final cigar presentation-so please complete and be ready to hand in the evaluation at the end. You may choose to add dessert or coffee, but it is not necessary. The total cost incurred for this event should be inclusive of food (consisting of the pasta bar and hors d'oeuvres) and possible room rental. If one hundred people attended and the costs were split between the three sponsors, each person's expenditure could be kept to under five hundred dollars and the mutual fund manager may pick up your share.

Other than the cigar smokers that you know, whom do you invite? Just ask the cigar merchant, the wine merchant and the food caterer for lists of their best clients. They all want to create deeper "mindshare" and they too need to appear unique to their clients. They will love the creativeness of your idea. Our experience is that you will get at least ten to twelve percent of the invitees to attend. A list of seven hundred will produce seventy to eighty attendees. Don't buy cigar

A purchased list from a list broker will produce a disappointment.

smoker names from a list broker. These people come because of relationships with the sponsors. A purchased list from a list broker will produce a disappointment. The sponsors have their own lists and they will participate. Oh...and don't forget where all the names go...into your *Prospect Fishbowl*.

Events are fun!

Our first cigar dinner attracted eighty-three attendees; thirty percent of the group was female. Only five of the attendees were past clients. The remaining attendees were people from the lists provided by the cigar and wine merchant. At the end of the evening, the evaluation forms indicated that over thirty attendees wanted to be contacted for the purpose of discussing financial issues pertaining specifically to them. Within six weeks, profits from new business exceeded total costs by over ten fold. The wine and cigar merchant were equally pleased with their results and wanted to repeat the event. If you are a cigar aficionado, you should repeat this event quarterly. Many attendees will return. People come back to "EVENTS." Events are fun! They are unlikely to come back to "SEMINARS." So here is a tip: Start calling your

Start calling your functions and seminars "events."

functions and seminars "events." Make them fun and watch them become popular and well attended. Even you will enjoy yourself more.

Cigar Smoker Dinner

Sample Agenda:

7:00 p.m.	Opening hors d'oeuvres	30 minutes
7:30	General Welcome	5 minutes
7:35	1st Cigar Introduction	15 minutes
7:50	1st Wine Presentation	10 minutes
8:00	1st Investment Strategy	12 minutes
8:12	PASTA BAR	45 minutes
	(Place evaluation forms at each table)	
9:00	Re-welcome – explain evaluation	
	form and end of evening drawings	3 minutes
9:03	2nd Investment Strategy	12 minutes
9:15	2nd Wine Presentation	10 minutes
9:25	2nd Cigar Presentation	15 minutes
9:40	Free Drawings	10 minutes
	(Collect evaluation forms)	
9:50	Conclusion – dessert and coffee optional	

Drawings:
1) 2 Bottles of wine
2) 4-6 Cigars
3) A book such as *The Millionaire Next Door,* by Dr. Thomas Stanley or *The Roaring 2000's,* by Harry Dent.

• Wine and cigars should be provided for free.

• Food should be split 3 ways. The caterer may provide it at cost.

• All attendee names should be given to all presenters, including the caterer, for their database.

• The reverse order of investment presentations and cigar presentations during the second part of the event will keep the attendees attentive and prevent early departures.

Should You Participate in Trade Shows?

Do any of your market segment groups have statewide annual trade shows? Consider participating (particularly if you have been published in their trade journal or newsletter), but instead of purchasing a booth to hand out boring company brochures and literature, ask to sponsor the coffee booth, at a cost usually no more than two hundred dollars. Hand out coffee in paper cups with your or your company's name printed on

Company brochures don't help!

them, and concentrate on greeting, meeting and making the attendees feel welcomed. Be an ambassador for the organization. Get to know the people. Get the attendees to give you their names and email addresses. Why? Take a digital camera and take candid photos of people in the exhibit area, promising to send the e-photo album to all the members, not just the attendees. Ask how the conference is going. Ask if you can assist with any of their needs. Announce that you are giving out candy bars at the breaks. A Snicker's or a Milky Way is received with a lot more enthusiasm than a Roth IRA brochure! You may even request a list of attendees from the organization and note the "friendly folks" as you talk with them. Your objective is to become "a little bit famous" and appreciated. Company brochures don't help!

If the organization is holding a golf tournament the day before the conference or trade show begins, DON'T GOLF IN THE TOURNAMENT! Instead, ask to sponsor the watering hole and follow the guidelines we gave to you just a few pages back.

If you do help sponsor their golf tournament, here's another idea for your trade booth that has been used with great success. Videotape portions of the golf tournament, such as each participant's golf drive when they arrive at your hole. Don't hire this to be done. The amateur approach is much funnier and the personal contacts you make are the significant point. When all the foursomes have passed by your hole, get into your golf cart, travel the course and take cameo videos of sand trap shots, their putting expertise and the fabulous chipping talent that gets displayed during these events. It can be pretty ugly but really funny. Play this video on a TV behind the coffee booth the next day. Trust me! You will not only attract the attendees, but the other exhibitors will wonder why they have no traffic and why everyone is staying at the coffee booth. You will be witnessing first hand how consumer preference is birthed! You are offering more than a brochure about your core product and service. It will pay off handsomely.

Trade Show Photo Album

Select at least two trade shows per year to attend. Purchase a trade show ticket and take a digital camera into the trade show. Approach each booth, hand them a business card and tell them, *"My name is (name) and I specialize in working with small business owners here in (city name). However, I am not here to introduce my services or to attempt to get an appointment – might be the high light of your day – a financial guy not asking for an appointment, huh? (wait for them to smile or chuckle). The reason I am here though, is to take a picture of your booth so we can send you a trade show photo album showing the fronts of everyone's booths. That way you can evaluate if you should adopt or adapt some of their ideas to help increase your booths attraction. My business clients always like this photo album and feel like it has been really helpful over the years. I am not only doing it for my clients, I am doing it for everyone this year. Can I get your picture here in the booth? And give me your business card and email address so I can send the album to you. You can download the pictures or just view it occasionally if you find a few ideas."*

No later than seven days after the event, send the e-photo album with the subject line: Trade Show Photo Album. It will get opened.

Robert E. Krumroy

One week later, send an e-Financial Storyboard to accentuate an area in which you specialize. Use the same subject line: Trade Show Photo Album. Start your message by saying, "Hopefully you will remember that I sent you the Trade Show Photo Album last week. This is just one way that we try to support our business clients, helping them find ways to increase profits. We have had a lot of nice comments and words of appreciation. If you remembered, I promised that I would send some occasional financial briefs on areas that our business clients find valuable. Here is one of those briefs. See if you would like the additional details. Just access the information below." Be ready for a lot of responses.

What market segment conferences or trade shows can you participate in?

Give Your VIPs Special Attention

Instead of sending your top twenty-five to forty clients birthday cards, identify these people as your VIP list and personally deliver a birthday cake to each of their offices. You can just drop by, or call the secretary first if you want to make sure that the VIP is there. This gesture and birthday recognition is cheaper than lunch and it has never happened to them. Never! Make your visit around 11:00 a.m. and watch who gets invited to lunch and who will insist on paying. The whole point is to look unique and distinctly different than the normal competition. Creating a superior value perception will require applying uniqueness and innovation. If you can look unique, not only will the business come your way but so will the referrals. You won't have to coerce the prospect for them either.

> *identify...your VIP list and personally deliver a birthday cake to each of their offices.*

What About CPA Referrals?

The question is always asked, "What about CPAs? I understand that they can be a great source of endorsements." Many CPA firms will eventually evaluate whether it is to their and their client's best advantage to create a financial service company alliance in order to offer financial planning. For CPA firms interested in sharing commissions or fees, the driving motivation is profits. Their choice as to whom they will develop this relationship with is important, but the final selection will be determined primarily on the thoroughness of the business proposal and their perception of competency. They will choose someone or some firm based on qualifications and not on friendship.

The CPA who desires a compensatory alliance will use a selection criterion that will differ from the CPA who does not want a compensatory arrangement. The most appealing compensatory arrangement for a CPA will provide complete details regarding all phases of the working relationship, samples of financial plans designed for clients, detailed profit projections and detailed explanations as to how you will support their new SEC compliance and supervisory roles. Compliance to a CPA is not a bad word. It is a comforting word. A CPA's job includes keeping their clients out of trouble. If you emphasize your support of compliance and offer to either handle or meaningfully assist in their new compliance supervisory responsibilities, you will gain a significant advantage over the competition that does not address it. Whether the CPA firm wants a compensatory or noncompensatory relationship, they all want proof of competency, objectivity and trust. Unless you have visibly established your local reputation and up-to-date capability by conducting local CPA continuing education courses, which almost anyone can register and conduct with a submitted outline to your state's CPA board, convincing a CPA firm that you should develop a formal shared client relationship will be difficult. A national company that will support these arrangements, assist the financial advisor with a thoroughly defined national program and include legal agreements, which must be signed by both parties, will create a perception of depth and safety that will have an even greater appeal to the CPA firm. In summary: Detailed formal structure, compliance assistance and legal agreements coupled with proven capabilities will be a winning combination. Now, let's address the CPA who wants to maintain the "purity of his or her profession" by keeping a taxation focus only, which many will choose as an option.

According to Russ Prince and Karen File, authors of the book *Marketing Through Advisors,* "36% of accountants made referrals of affluent clients to life insurance professionals in the last year." However, there is a catch. In order for you to effectively position yourself to win over advisors, you will need to become an expert at creating among these advisors awareness about yourself, your practice and the services you provide. According to Prince and File in their interviews with CPAs, most agents make the mistake of looking for a referral-handout every time they are with their CPA (90.8%). CPAs are unanimously unappreciative of this (0.0%) and they do not regard it as an effective way

> *most agents make the mistake of looking for a handout every time they are with their CPA*

to build the relationship. The goal should be to provide value. Display your expertise by giving private, quarterly CE seminars at their firm. Conducting CE seminars at colleges or libraries for the entire CPA community to attend is not nearly as affective. No one will ask questions and they certainly won't ask about a client – both of which will occur if the seminars are held in the privacy of their own firm. Print a yearly index card listing the subjects of your quarterly CE seminars. Get on your CPA's quarterly schedule for four 7 am – 9 am sessions throughout the year. Offer to bring doughnuts and ask them to provide coffee. Continually maintain constant connection, asking how you can help with their needs. Finally, become friends. Find a CPA in a firm that you genuinely like and start the process. Be patient and don't ask for referrals. Advisors are well aware that you would appreciate leads. When the time comes, if you have captured the "mindshare," you will be rewarded often. Just remember, this is a long-term project. Be consistent in maintaining quarterly contact by providing CE opportunities in their office and patient in giving the process adequate time to yield results.

The CPA Lunch And Bagel Connection – The BIG Impact

CPAs can lead you into a lot of business, but creating knowledge in your area of expertise, along with trust and likability is a process that takes time and strategy. Create a list of CPAs (at least 25) that you would like to build a relationship with. On the busiest day of the year, which is the day before tax deadline, April 14, August 14 (day before the first extension date), and October 14 (day before the last extension date), take box lunches to their office. A turkey and havarti croissant, cookie, chips and an apple cost about $5. If you want to vary the menu take a bagel platter in August and doughnuts, breakfast biscuits or a cookie tray in October. These encounters will surprise and delight them, which is always the first element of getting attention. Don't have a catering company deliver the food. Do it personally. Clear your schedule for April 15 so you can receive the numerous thank you calls. Also, don't expect a huge onslaught of business after your first endeavor. It has happened, but be patient. You can expect some serious referrals after doing this consistently for a year. Paper clip your business card to a pre-printed note and insert it into each lunch. Here is the example of the note:

We both know that today is a very taxing day on the average citizen in America, however, I also know that today's work load makes it a very taxing day on you – which may make it difficult for you to get out for lunch or even dinner. I hope that this snack pack helps in that regards and expresses my appreciation for your work and contribution to my clients, many of whom we share though we have never discussed. Many of my clients express their appreciation of their CPAs, often commenting about the trust and prudent advice they receive. Again, my thanks for the value that you deliver, it makes a difference. If I can ever provide information on insurance, investments or employee benefit packages, please feel free to ask. It is always a pleasure hearing from my CPA friends and clients.

Sincerely,
(Your Name)
(Your Phone Number)

REMEMBER – creating a lasting local market presence, one that outclasses the competition, requires CONSISTENCY. One-time events don't build BIG results. It's what you do consistently, that makes a personal impact that eventually places YOU on the tip of their minds - and builds BIG results. Agents who deliver lunches on April 14th, follow up with bagels on August 14th and doughnuts, breakfast biscuits or a cookie tray on October 14th eventually see their efforts pay off in a BIG way – many reporting major sales increases from CPA referrals who call them. Great alliance-relationships evolve by initiating touch-points that create "linkage to the heart" and differentiate YOU from the competition. Wondering what to say if you choose to do the follow-up bagel delivery on August 14th? Try the following:

Dear CPA,

August 14th is always a BIG DAY in the life of a CPA - a day similar to April 14th. I know that today's workload can consume about every minute of your available time. How do I know? A lot of my financial work includes working with the CPA, in coordination with my clients. It is how I prefer to work, especially with my more affluent clients.

Why the bagels? Hopefully these bagels will again say "thanks" for the value you give to my clients, many of whom we unknowingly share. If I can ever provide you with information about insurance, insurance funding techniques, qualified plans or other financial issues, please give me a call. It is always good hearing from my CPA friends. Enjoy the bagels.

Branding YOU as distinctly different and preferred in your market requires more than just an occasional seminar or a sporadic lunch. It requires multiple and consistent connection that is exceptionally different than what the competition delivers. Be different! Exceptionally different! Be consistent! Stay visible! The eventual results will be far greater than the effort exerted.

What CPA firm(s) should I contact and begin cultivating a relationship with?

What About a Property & Casualty Alliance?

An alliance between a property and casualty firm and a life insurance professional, or a financial advisor, is potentially one of the most profitable alliances that either party can form. However, it is also one of the hardest alliances to achieve due to the perception of differences in goals and objectives of each organization. Unless those perceptions can be addressed up front, the success of putting together an alliance, much less making one last, will be limited or completely lacking.

Before addressing the challenges and how to overcome them, both parties together should review the benefits of an alliance and decide if they are complementary to their business goals. There are four major benefits for creating an alliance that are worthy of consideration.

Four Benefits of Creating a Successful Property & Casualty Alliance

1. An alliance can help both organizations spread or avoid costs while providing a new business channel for increasing profits.

2. P&C companies gain an enhanced respect from their customers if they promote that they are extending a new service by forming a link with a specialist. It implies that they are maintaining a narrow focus to maintain a higher level of expertise in their field than their competitors. They are also acknowledging that they are addressing their customers' additional needs with an equally higher level of expertise than an "all service" organization would be capable of providing. This "endorsement" of sorts increases the customers' perception of specialized expertise and high level of client concern.

3. Each party gains an immediate credibility with those customers that they share when needs arise. Trust is passed on and, therefore, must be honored as "an entrusted gift to be handled with the utmost respect by the recipient."

4. Creating a deeper client loyalty through alliance marketing will help insulate the client from competitors, as well as direct-selling attempts from competing companies in the new technology age of marketing. The more commodity-like your product is, the easier it becomes to "price shop." P&C coverage is an easier target for direct-marketing attacks than a creative deferred compensation executive benefit plan is. However, unless the parties create an emotional bond with the client, the client remains vulnerable to outside direct database marketing pursuits.

Roman G Hiebing, Jr. and Scott W. Cooper, authors of *The One-Day Marketing Plan,* say, "It is harder for competitors to attack emotional relationships than specific product attributes once a relationship is established." Additionally, most consumers are less concerned about "better and best" in today's world of product proliferation and far more concerned with keeping things simple. That is why brands, according to Harry Beckwith, author of *Selling the Invisible,* account for ninety-three percent of all products purchased by consumers. Brands offer a perception of safety. Within today's society of information overload, we are less concerned about our brand choice being the best, whether choosing a consumable product or a service professional, than we are about insulating ourselves from new information that challenges our past conclusions. Insulating ourselves from challenging information allows us to simplify our lives. Kevin J. Clancy and Robert S. Shulman, authors of *Marketing Myths That Are Killing Business* agree: "Consumers no longer feel the need to buy the "best"...products; they are saying that there are better things to do with their time and money." In doing their research, they found that the majority of consumers agreed with the statement, "I don't have time to investigate the quality of different brands…" All of this supports the conclusion that, once a strong relationship bond is formed with a client, the relationship will withstand most product challenges.

With the array of product choices in the market place today and the constant onslaught of marketing attacks, it is imperative that an emotional bond with your client be formed and continually nurtured. Bonded relationships begin with a personal experience and are maintained in the same way.

in the market place today…it is imperative that an emotional bond with your client be formed and continually nurtured.

The more frequent the contact, the more solid the bond. When a strategic alliance is successful, the perceived depth of expertise is enhanced and the contact frequency is increased, all of which creates a deeper commitment to the chosen brand. Everyone wins, but most important, the client benefits.

With all the benefits available to both parties from structuring an alliance, why does it seem so difficult to initiate and maintain it? There are four major obstacles that must be overcome.

Four Property & Casualty Alliance Obstacles That Must Be Overcome

1. Perceived loss of control by the P&C firm

2. Fear of losing a client due to the other party's behavior

3. Being represented by someone who does not share the same value for their client base that they spent years to build

4. Poor communication

All of these obstacles can be resolved if both parties will take the time to openly discuss their concerns. Usually, the greatest fears are on the P&C side and rightfully so. The majority of their income is renewal income in contrast to the life agent's first-year commission stream. Regardless of the life agent's sincere insistence that he or she values their clients, the compensation difference is a troublesome issue for the P&C firm. It can cause an easy jump to the conclusion that sales, and not service, are the number-one concern. That is the first roadblock that must be circumvented. Acknowledge the fact that you will never resolve this issue in the beginning with one hundred percent comfort. It will only resolve itself over time as both parties view the actions of each other. However, there are some steps that can be taken to add some degree of comfort for the P&C firm.

Most P&C firms are going to be resistant to opening their entire files to the life agent without any control. On the other hand, it is unrealistic for the P&C firm to think that the client will

you can jointly send a systematic communication, a joint e-newsletter, to the client...

somehow contact them when he or she is ready for a buy-sell, a deferred compensation plan, an age-weighted profit-sharing plan or even a simple mutual fund or a financial plan. It simply won't happen. What can happen is that you can jointly send a systematic communication, email works great, to the client that provides educational information, not product solicitation, on a regular basis. This communication must give the client the ability to easily respond when they want more details. This same database of clients should also be invited to attend periodic and unique events. Build an Identity Brand together as a team. Develop a client contact plan and stick to it. Once the relationship starts to take hold, the P&C firm will become more receptive to discussing clients that they feel should be proactively contacted. Give it time.

If you do a regular educational-type email communication (which to be effective should go out at least eight times per year), allow the client responses to go directly back to the P&C firm. Remember, one of the largest roadblocks was control. The P&C firm can then review them and decide how much control they want to maintain when the contact is made, such as requesting that a meeting be scheduled jointly or that it be held in their office. The life insurance agent, or financial advisor, needs to be responsible for the mailing, but the control of replies and the initial contact decision should be offered to the P&C firm. Once this relationship develops, you will see increasing cooperation. The P&C firm will delegate more and more authority as their confidence builds that you have their best interest at heart and not your own pocketbook.

> *The sales professional's job...helping to develop the "Brand" reputation of the P&C firm, not their own.*

A further word of caution: Ask the P&C firm if they want the client mailing to show the agent's or financial advisor's name or if they prefer to simply indicate that a strategic alliance with a "business market center" or an "estate specialist" has been formed. Arguing about putting the sales professional's name on the client mailing can stop an alliance discussion almost immediately. The sales professional's job in the relationship should be viewed as helping to develop the "Brand" reputation of the P&C firm, not their own. The sales professional should be focused on giving additional value recognition to the P&C firm's special needs as an enhancement to the P&C firm's reputation, rather than as a way to "get" more clients. That will happen as a result of focusing on "giving," instead of focusing on "getting." If you help the P&C firm get what they want, they will eventually help you get more than you ever expected. Building a solid relationship with a P&C firm is like maintaining a good marriage. Once you have initiated the discussion about forming an alliance, don't let it be you who gives them a reason to leave.

What P&C firm should I approach about an alliance/branding relationship?

Don't Confuse Target Selling With Target Marketing

Many sales professionals and managers confuse target selling with target marketing. Not only are the two distinctly different, but eventually their paths will take you to two different destinations. Target marketing, when done correctly, allows you to become Identity Branded within an emotionally cohesive group of people who have the financial means to complement your talent capability. In other words, if your talent capability allows you to apply your skill level to the sophisticated executive compensation market, you would eventually become highly discouraged if your daily routine was working with young married couples. Even if you could increase your income, you would eventually become dissatisfied and bored because you would be underemployed. Your skill level would be underutilized.

> *Identity Branding "who you are"…creates consumer pull…attraction*

Marketing, by individualizing your *Prospect Fishbowl*, allows you to evolve your prospects upward by adding some and eliminating others over time. Furthermore, Identity Branding "who you are" to your prospects, creates consumer pull. Ultimately, it creates a compelling attraction where the consumer not only accepts your request for an appointment but actually wants to meet with you.

Conversely, an example of target selling may be getting yourself in front of a group of people who have little commonality but somehow got placed together in a meeting or seminar. You may have convinced a large employer to allow you to do a series of seminars for their employees. They may have even approved a payroll deduction option for their employees. If this is your intended business strategy, such as focusing on voluntary benefits through group enrollment, fine. If not, you may meet your sales or commission goal but the majority of your sales may not utilize your talents. If that's the case, as your educational development continues you may eventually feel trapped within a nonchallenging market. You will realize that not only do you have limited access to the higher income markets that you are capable of handling, but you have no "mindshare" of the prospects you desire to contact. Your focus has been directed elsewhere. This is the unfortunate result and final destination of building one's business from a selling model, versus a marketing model.

Another example of target selling, versus target marketing, is the sales professional who calls on newly married couples, new mortgage leads, new births, newly retired people and even newly formed businesses (with no other identifying characteristic). You may get some sales, but the market characteristics of commonality, frequent communication and shared purpose between the individuals, which make up the definition of a market segment, are probably nonexistent. If this is an initial effort to accumulate potential prospects for familiarization within your *Prospect Fishbowl*, which later can be sorted out to fit your talent level, your efforts may serve a valuable purpose (depending on the amount of time this strategy takes). There is nothing wrong with introducing new prospects to your *Prospect Fishbowl* that initially add intrigue, even if you are not sure that they initially fit. If the cultivation cost and time to acquire these names is hardly noticeable, you may end up pleasantly surprised, but immediately discard names that you find do not match your prospect profile or your talent level. If your efforts at target selling to a loosely defined market, even if through seminars, are just to drive sales results from any breathing prospect, eventually you will stop regardless of your commission success. You will find no sustaining career fulfillment. You will quit, go to a different company, or become motivationally stalled and reach a production plateau.

A prospect attraction focus builds your future. A target selling focus may provide immediate income, but it will not provide the motivation to stay the course. Neither will you feel any more secure three years from now in this business. You will still be wondering where your next sale will come from. You will know that you have captured no "mindshare" within any particular prospect market and you will be keenly aware that you have no unique prospect attraction relative to the competition.

Attraction-marketing is not just something you do to get into the door; it determines the long-term satisfaction that you will derive from your efforts. It is what sustains the personal feelings of accomplishment. The sales professionals who build their business from a prospect attraction marketing platform, versus a selling platform, will find a prospect community that will appreciate them, acknowledge their character and generously reward them with their business. You will be regarded as one who gives generously of themselves, and the prospect community will generously give back.

> *sales professionals...who build their business from an attraction-marketing platform, versus a selling platform...are generously rewarded.*

Markets to Avoid

A word of caution may help you avoid focusing your marketing efforts on organizations that will eventually prove to be disappointing. Don't focus your marketing efforts on non-cohesive organizations that people join because others "expect them to join" or to groups that they might be members of for only a short period of time, i.e., the Better Business Bureau, your child's school PTA. Some of these organizations may be cohesive in smaller towns, and may prove to be good choices, but in larger towns, where being a member may be expected, your membership carries no weight when influencing someone to do business with you. This is not a commentary on the value or importance of these groups. Many of these organizations play a vital role within your community and should be supported with your membership dollars. However, a group that you will want to choose as a market segment focus must have members who want to sincerely be affiliated, want to contribute to the cause and the cause must have a lasting place in their hearts. Just ask yourself if most members would look forward to attending a holiday social, hosted by the group. If not, you have limited cohesiveness. The board of directors and officers may be cohesive, but that is not adequate for making an impact on the market segment if the majority of the group is emotionally uninvolved. Doing business with one member will have no influence on another member's opinion of you. In other words, you will be unable to create market preference within this group.

Some Other "Don'ts!"

Are there things that you shouldn't do, things that will probably just be a waste of money and time? Yes! Don't purchase exhibitor space in a community tradeshow, i.e., the city's annual business expo, the home living show, the Christmas/holiday show. Remember, we are focusing on building our business on an attraction-marketing model, not a selling model. We want to build a prospect highway that continuously provides welcomed access to a prospect community and utilizes your skill level, not just do things for making another sale. If your group is noncohesive and weakly defined, your efforts will not help create a specific market segment that provides a prospect highway to prospects with consumer attraction. As Dan Kennedy says in *The Ultimate Marketing Plan*, "…every business …appeals much more strongly to a certain definable group of people than

> *build a prospect highway that continuously provides welcomed access to a prospect community and utilizes your skill level…*

it appeals to all people." If you attempt to appeal to everyone, you will appeal to no one. You probably won't even appeal to YOUR-SELF.

A community trade show attracts a group of people that is too general. The show's theme of fishing, home improvement or boats has nothing in common with the typical financial advisor. The cellular phone exhibition booth, though not what the attendees came to see, may attract some interest. Cellular phones are a commodity and are used daily by a lot of people, but no one is carrying around his or her insurance policy or investment portfolio in hopes that someone will be occupying a booth at the home show where they can get a pressing financial question answered. It is no wonder why you will have disappointing results in a general trade show. You can find better ways to spend marketing dollars.

Don't include an insurance solicitation to your clients due to their age increase with a birthday card or within a birthday letter. Believe it or not, the word is out. They know that the letter is intended to get new business much more than to convey a sincere birthday wish. If you want to send birthday wishes, leave the business stuff out!

Don't purchase a general prospect list from a list broker to get your *Prospect Fishbowl* project underway. Buying a list is a lazy alternative to finding markets where you share a social of belief connection. There will be no cohesiveness in a purchased list. It will be impossible to become a little bit famous. A purchased list will prove disastrous for putting together a lasting market that provides continued growth and personal satisfaction.

Don't purchase a general prospect list from a list broker to get your Prospect Fishbowl project underway.

Endorsements or Referrals?...Both!

Building an effective prospect foundation, a *Prospect Fishbowl*, is the culmination of identifying a market segment(s) and then individualizing the prospects so that you can create a favorable impact in order to create preference, a superior value perception and a competitive advantage. If you don't obtain and know the individual names of your prospects, this would be an impossible task. Your objective is to eventually "own" the market segment, not just a "market share." The ultimate goal is to create a perception of distinction and differentiation, to become the professional of choice to an identified market.

While you are identifying your market segment and creating your *Prospect Fishbowl*, you will want to gather names from observation, personal involvement within the market segment and from referrals and endorsements given to you by other people. Although your focus of "gathering names" will eventually change to "migrating" among the market, you will always want to maintain your effort to continually upgrade your *Prospect Fishbowl* with new names. If you don't, you will eventually find that your skill level exceeds your market access level and your enthusiasm, plus your income will be limited. Continually adding prospects to your *Prospect Fishbowl* is imperative. It allows you to eliminate prospects that don't fit your skill level without fear of depleting your selling opportunities by reducing the quantity of potential prospects. At the same time, it allows you to upgrade your *Prospect Fishbowl* with better prospects that utilize your skill level more frequently and builds your competency and confidence.

you will always want to maintain your effort to continually upgrade your Prospect Fishbowl with new names

One of the ways of upgrading your *Prospect Fishbowl* is through the acquisition of referrals and endorsements. Both sources require the participation of someone who regards you favorably. The higher the regard for who you are, or the higher your perception as the "Brand of Choice" (Identity Brand) within your market segment, the greater the likelihood that you will be successful in this endeavor.

Referrals are simply names of prospects attained from an individual who felt comfortable enough to provide them. Getting referrals of any significant magnitude always requires a conscious and proactive effort. It happens because you make it happen. Those who don't get referrals, have only themselves to fault. Referrals do not just come on their own, regardless of your length of time in business or your prestige in the community. They come because you ask.

> *Getting referrals...requires a conscious and proactive effort. It happens because you make it happen.*

When you get into a discussion about referrals, always identify your prospect profile to the referrer so that the names fit your skill level. If you aren't always protective of your ideal prospect profile you will violate it. If you aren't protective, even if, by accident, you will find yourself getting involved working with prospects that are below your skill level and you will limit your income potential.

One way of maintaining the integrity of your prospect profile is to carry a laminated card the size of a business card that lists the two most important characteristics of your profile, plus the number of referrals you are requesting. As your experience, age and specialization in your field change, you will find that your prospect profile will change as well. Usually, the most important criteria of any prospect profile are income - whether it is individual or family, net worth - if you are working the estate or investment market, and market segment affiliation. The only exceptions are if you are working a product-specific specialty where the product requires certain buyer criteria such as an age requirement for long-term care insurance or business ownership for 401(k) retirement plans. Other criteria are dependent on the market segment that you are trying to penetrate, personal preference or the requirements that you need to maintain for the narrower focus of a proclaimed specialty.

One of the reasons that laminated cards listing your prospect profile work so well is that the majority of people in the world are

the majority of people in the world are "visually oriented."

"visually oriented."They would rather see a map than read written directions. They would rather see a demonstration, how something is done, rather than read or hear about how it should be done. The best managers of new people in any organization always couple "in-house" training with "field experience" that shows the new skill. New attorneys watch senior attorneys. New waitresses and waiters follow around experienced ones to see demonstrated what they have been taught, how to serve customers. Your best result in getting what you want is to "show them." Hand them the profile-card and let them feel it and see it while they think. Include the number of referrals that you want to obtain on the card. Implementing this one idea will bring to you a new level of success in obtaining referrals.

You may also want to use a referral duplication form for recording referral names, promising to give them a copy when you leave. This provides an assurance for the referrer that you value his or her input and respect the importance of these names. You may suggest that he or she call these people before you do or promise that you will include them on a regular e-newsletter-mailing program for a period of time before contacting them. The duplication form is another reminder to emphasize to the referrer the prospect profile that you are seeking. Since the desired prospect characteristics are printed on the form, it is hard for either one of you to stray off the intended profile.

Following are examples of laminated cards and the referral duplication form.

Laminated Referral Cards

Business Owner / Professional
Income > $100,000
3 Names

Executive / Professional
Family Income > $90,000
4 Names

Referral Duplication Form

Business Owner / Professional
Income _____

Name _____   Name _____

Phone _____   Phone _____

Info _____   Info _____

Name _____   Name _____

Phone _____   Phone _____

Info _____   Info _____

Name _____   Name _____

Phone _____   Phone _____

Info _____   Info _____

Name _____   Name _____

Phone _____   Phone _____

Info _____   Info _____

In choosing your market segment(s), if you have focused on and share the common denominators of the segment, which are cohesiveness, usually reflected by an occupational, lifestyle, social, or ethnic commonality, and the members maintain consistent communication between each other, you have a tremendous opportunity for attaining endorsements. Your personal commonality, in combination with the other denominators, gives you a significant advantage. If you have identified and influenced an "individualized" market segment by "giving" and not just "getting," the endorsement route is your most effective means for upgrading your *Prospect Fishbowl* as well as eventually gaining market access to desirable prospects.

Endorsements are the reverse of referrals and are usually the best method of maintaining the integrity of your prospect profile and in working within your skill level. It is simply the act of providing a name that you already have in your *Prospect Fishbowl*, which fits your prospect profile, and asking the referring person for information about the person and an endorsement to be used when you call on him or her. Your request

Endorsements are...the best method of...working within your skill level.

should be similar to: *"Jack, here is a list of names (in the market segment that this person is familiar with) that I currently send e-newsletters to on a regular basis and invite to special events. Eventually, I will call on each one of them and I hope, over a period of time, a number of them will become clients. Could you take a minute and tell me whom I should call on first and, probably just as important, whom I should avoid. Your insights would be really valuable."*

Clearly state that you will eventually be calling on each one of them. You are not asking for a name. You are asking for information about the people you are going to call on. You even ask for those whom the referrer thinks would be a waste of time.

That doesn't mean that you will remove them from your *Prospect Fishbowl*. You may find someone later who is this person's best friend and provides an incredible introduction, but it is amazing how many people will find it easy to start talking about who they don't like, and why, and then feel that they have to give you names of "good people" that you should call on just to redeem themselves. Let the referrer go in any direction he or she wants. You both will have fun. When the referrer is done, ask if you can mention his or her name when you call the prospect. Since you were the initiator of the name, permission is always granted.

What About the Effect of the Internet?

Bill Gates, Microsoft founder and one of the wealthiest men in the world today, said that you don't have to be able to predict the future, but you sure better pay attention to where it's headed. Wayne Gretsky, the greatest hockey player in history, was asked what had defined his remarkable playing career. He said that he learned early not to skate to where the puck was but to skate to where the puck was going to be. Well, you also need to start skating not to where the market is but to where the "marketplace will be" as Lynn B. Upshaw, author of *Building Brand Identity,* says. It will be the only game in town. It's a game of single elimination. If you lose this one, just go home. There are no prizes for second place.

> *you need to start skating not to where the market is but to where the "marketplace will be"*

Yes, the Internet will affect YOU and THIS business, not just everyone else. Someday in the future the Internet will be accessible from everyone's cable TV box and all computers will be voice friendly, allowing your clients to converse with you face-to-face. The technology is already available.

Is it possible that in the near future infomercials won't advertise a telephone number in order to be able to talk to the psychic hotline? You will be able to simply point the infrared TV changer to the "contact us" square on the screen and be connected with your personal sales person in a face-to-face chat, a personal relationship!

In the next ten years, a lot of traditional appointments in which one drives to the other's office or home, will be eliminated. If I, the consumer, want to avoid further intrusion during my nonworking hours, I will ask that we meet over the Internet to discuss what you are proposing. To prosper, the sales professional of the future will learn to conduct many of his or her interviews by this means. You can look at this change as an opportunity or a problem. Different sales professionals will view it differently, but all who survive will have to adapt.

it won't be just term insurance that gets sold over the Internet

What are the problems and threats that this new technology will represent to you? First of all, it won't be just term insurance that gets sold over the Internet. When companies can contact prospects through call centers with a face-to-face encounter over the Internet, they will definitely capture a larger portion of market share. Companies will have rooms of cubicles filled with marketers in their national headquarters (e-commerce technology calls them "Customer Relationship Management Centers). Those marketers' job will be to make face-to-face contact with their customers for either service or "good will" and then attempt to cross sell other products. What we refer to today, as alternative distribution channels, will create a major impact. If shares in your financial company are publicly traded on the stock exchange, obtaining business by e-commerce (Internet) will not be a choice! Sooner or later, a lack of e-commerce will hurt the company's credibility and their stock price. E-commerce must become a significant distribution channel for attaining increased profits and return on equity (ROE). The methods employed by these companies for attaining this business will become highly creative.

> *obtaining business by e-commerce (Internet) will not be a choice!*

How many of your clients have a major credit card from a company that, in the future, will offer "financial planning" advice? It will be an easy task for companies to access their own client base over the Internet. Think about American Express and how many of your clients have their card. Would you want to bet on whether a customer relationship manager contacts them about annuities or investment products through interactive technology over the Internet, on their TV screen, within the next ten years? What about the banks whose customers are also yours and have now merged with insurance companies? Your clients, as well as prospects, will have numerous opportunities to personally interface with people competing for what you thought was your business. The contacts will be over the Internet. The consumer will now have an alternative to a living, walking, breathing salesperson.

Just last week my credit card company called to communicate that they had noticed unusual activity on my credit card and wanted to verify that it wasn't stolen. They noticed charges from out of the country and as a courtesy, were calling to verify that these were indeed my charges. After I verified that they were indeed mine, I was then led through a discussion about their credit card protection plan and asked to sign up. After that, I was asked about other credit card balances that I might want to transfer to them based on their new promotional rate. Do you really think that this all started due to a "courtesy call" to verify charges, or due to a planned and intentional cross-selling corporate strategy? Imagine that in the near future, during a "courtesy call," they will ask if they can send an email package on financial planning and products that may be of interest. A lot of people will say, "yes" to that offer. A follow-up phone call from a technology communication "specialist" (a customer relationship manager) a week later may provide some rather amazing results.

I am sure that companies will eventually send email information packages to all of their clients as the company databases become more refined. Database mining makes it easy to pinpoint prospects with newly available cash - families who have a child finally getting out of college, a home mortgage being paid off or a large gain on a stock transaction. Once identified, you can attain response levels to investment messages higher than ever imagined. Database marketing will eventually affect your entire market and all consumers. It will even be used by charitable organizations to

> *I am sure that companies will eventually send email information packages to all...clients*

determine the best time to solicit someone about a sizeable contribution. They will be able to see the financial signals that indicate that "now" is the best predictive time to make the solicitation contact.

Calls from these customer relationship managers to your clients are not courtesy calls. They are creative strategy calls for directly cross-selling their other products. And the email introduction packages are not just introduction packages; they are interactive programs that allow you to click on a reply icon to request more specific information, a comparison or a quote. You will see what used to be dubbed "computer phone bank" operations now set up as "Relationship Management Centers" in major companies. Licensed operators, trained in how to sell and how to effectively handle the email and interactive responses, will staff them. Ask GEICO if it works. It will work even better when you are able to make an initial contact that appears to be a "high concern" relationship contact about the prospect's personal credit card safety or some other creative issue. Your clients and prospects are going to be pursued by many new players. E-commerce will be a distribution channel in most, if not all, companies that will be accountable for producing significant results. The communication technology will not replace personal relationships; it will provide an appealing alternative, a "direct contact" personal relationship. The cover story on *Business Week,* June 28, 1999, said, "Any company that relies on a traditional sales force will have to do some soul searching…companies are finding that they need new skills…" I would suggest that the individual sales professional needs new skills as well.

So, what is the positive side of technology? Can there be advantages for the local salesperson derived through this new medium of com-

you…better start deciding "HOW", not if, you will use the Internet in your marketing efforts

munication? The answer is yes! In the magazine, *Strategy and Business,* Fourth Quarter 1999, an article entitled "The Internet as a Marketing Medium", Frank Ingari, comments that companies better begin recognizing that "…the web is likely to be the center of their marketing future, not simply an adjunct to traditional marketing methods." The issue is that you, the sales associate, as well as the companies, better start deciding "HOW", not if, you will use the Internet in your marketing efforts. Dan Sullivan, author of *The 21st Century Agent,* writes, "…those who operate as entrepreneurs and who use micro technology to their competitive advantage will succeed." He goes on to say, "The entire global economy is going electronic faster than anyone can comprehend…the ability to navigate within this universe and to create value…is now the key to personal and professional success…"

Internet technologies will neither replace all sales professionals nor make them dispensable, but it will produce a major change in the way you will have to conduct business. The Internet may, in fact, be the sales professional's best way to stay current, communicate and sell more to their clients. The traditional argument that "face-to-face contact can never be replaced with anything that will get the same results and, therefore, I need not concern myself" is too simplistic in today's market place.

There will always be clients and prospects, termed "relationship delegators," who will want a local sales professional, but even these people will want a sales professional that can save them time by occasionally accessing them with a face-to-face encounter over the Internet, instead of always in person. The day will come when many will regard this ability as critical in their choice of establishing or even maintaining a business relationship with you. The very least a client or prospect will expect is your ability to send an email information package on the new idea that you want to discuss with them as well as any other general information, announced events and e-newsletters. This is all available today! The prospect's condition of entry into the relationship will be your ability to communicate with them via the Internet/communication systems. This is not an issue that you can afford to ignore. Clients and prospects are no longer patient while you are catching up. They don't need to be. There are lots of new alternatives. Today's consumer wants what they want, when they want it and they expect you to provide it. You don't have to be able to predict the future but, as Peter Drucker says, "We must pay attention to survive."

Technology and Identity Branding your personal reputation to your individualized, local markets are not mutually exclusive, rather they are complementary. One without the other will not meet the needs of the future client. Together, they can capture market share and increase productivity. The following story may help you to visualize this new future.

A Story From The Future

It's a day in the future. Jack just got home from work. The competition on the job is more and more intense. Every company seems to want more and more out of less and less to increase their profit margins in order to stay competitive. After dinner, Jack goes to the Web TV. Although introduced in June of 2000, it didn't really catch on until years later. It is amazing how it has evolved over the last three years. Jack uses it all the time for almost everything. Most people do. The Internet is now part of the basic service cost for cable TV so there is no longer a separate cost for accessing the Internet. It's been like that for five years now. And the interactive shopping channels make it so easy to buy almost anything that you need. They only require pointing the remote control and a quick "click." Jack has agreed to be interviewed on how the Internet changed his and his family's life. Here are a few excerpts from that interview.

*Q: **Tell me how Internet communication has affected your family.***

A: Well, we use it for everything now, shopping, vacations, groceries, talking to our friends, etc. It is also the first thing that any of us check whenever we have been away from the house or when I get home every evening, kind of like how you used to check your telephone answering machines. Wow, that's showing my age, isn't it? Now that your phone messages connect through the Internet, it's so much easier to see who called before you even retrieve the message. You can prioritize how you pick them up or which ones you just discard. Even my Mom and Dad use it with all of their friends, now. It is so easy to use, especially since it is connected through the TV cable.

*Q: **What are some other examples of how Internet access via TV has influenced your family.***

A: I can sure tell you that Mom, who is 76 years old, has caught on. I guess with learning to use the ATM machines at the bank she finally figured out that her favorite show, QVC shopping network, wasn't any more complicated. She says that it became even more fun to watch once she could "click" and buy. I think she is addicted. She still marvels at how they merged the TV, phone and computer all into one. She used to be afraid of the "computer in the box." Now, it's just part of her TV and easy to use!

Q: What about your dad? Does he use Internet TV also?

A: Oh, man, my Dad thinks it's great that he can talk to the travel agent over the TV set now and plan his and Mom's next trip. He planned a trip with Mom to London last year and by the time he was done communicating with the travel agent on TV, I think he made a new best friend. He even talks to his stockbroker like that now. They talk and view stock charts together over the TV. He is a little embarrassed when he sees his former broker at church, but that guy just never adapted to the new technology. To make the trips over to his former broker's office just got to be too inconvenient. And Dad hates people coming to his home to sell stuff to him. Actually, I think that everyone does. Anyway, Dad loves this new Web TV technology. I'm not even sure that his former broker is in the business anymore. You know, I don't think he was old enough to have retired. Oh, well…I guess things just happen.

Q: Were you surprised that your parents adapted so quickly to Web TV?

A: Who would have ever guessed that the older generation would take to this like they did. I guess we never thought about the mobility issues that this technology resolved or how easy it would become to use. Dad even does the grocery shopping now. He loves the virtual shopping aisles that he wheels his virtual shopping cart down and then the pointing and clicking. Plus, they credit his bill with all the national coupons (check out: Lowesfoodtogo.com – It is all available NOW!). I think he feels like he is in control. Oh, yeah, he always talks to the Internet grocer, even if to just say hi. You'd think that they were also best friends. Who ever thought that relationships would be easier to develop on the Internet than in person? Well, I guess they are communicating in person aren't they?

Q: *Have they bought a lot of other products or services over the Web TV?*

A: *He told me that the other day his insurance company, that is now part of The Big National Bank, contacted him through email over his TV. I think they issue his credit card, too. Anyway, I don't really know who called him, the bank, the insurance company or the credit card people. Nevertheless, it was a face-to-face, good-will service contact by TV email. Pretty cool! They sent him an interactive email presentation through the TV on some information that he could click through. He liked it and clicked on the request block to talk to a representative to answer some questions. The representative was on Web TV within seconds! Dad really*

> Who ever thought that relationships would be easier to develop on the Internet than in person?

liked the guy, said he was as personable as his agent, plus it was just so convenient to talk personally over the TV. He didn't even have to leave a message for the guy to get back to him. Don't you hate having to leave voice mails and hope someone will call you back? This was instantaneous. That is hard to beat.

Q: Is his insurance agent still around?

A: Oh, his agent is still around, but he doesn't think that his agent will ever find out that he purchased an annuity from this TV guy. Plus, it's just a business deal. It's not that he doesn't like him anymore; he does. But it's not like his agent is an old college roommate or they see each other a lot. He also told this Web TV representative to contact me with information on a college education fund for the new twins. Dad is always trying to help. I guess that never ends.

Q: Did the guy call you?

A: Yes. He did call. He seems like a really nice guy. I told him that I worked with a financial planner and he said that was usually the norm, but then he asked if he could send me an

> he asked if he could send me an interactive email package over the Internet

interactive email package over the Internet that I could click through that might provide some helpful information on college planning.

Q: And did he send it?

A: Oh yeah… and it was great! I didn't have to go to a Web site. It just came through on my email screen. It allowed me to click through five or six pages. I was impressed with all the information I could access so easily. (Note: These are available now. Go to www.e-relationship.com) He called me back about a week later and we talked over Web TV so that we could see each other plus the information at the same time. He said that most of their clients really like reviewing stuff like this in this way and that they had been doing it for about four years now. You know, they have got to be a great company to be this advanced.

Q: What about your financial planner?

A: My planner is a really good guy, but I just don't have the time to make a face-to-face appointment, as my planner always wants me to. I wonder why my guy doesn't contact me like this. I guess that most local agents all work pretty much the same. Not very hi-tech, huh? Makes you wonder if maybe their company isn't very up-to-date either. You know, years ago he told me that I would always want a personal agent but between these interactive email packages and Web TV, you can't get much more personal.

personal agent but between these interactive email packages and Web TV, you can't get much more personal. You know, he should really start doing this or he could lose a lot of business, don't you think?

Q: Why did you say that the company might not be up-to-date and not just the agent?

A: Well, I think they're a good company. They are one of the top ten in size, anyway. But I only get US Mail from them on everything. It's inconvenient, irritating and harder to reply, versus just clicking on a reply link to an Internet message. Why don't they use the Internet to communicate? It just doesn't make sense. Sure, they have a Web site, but who cares! Everyone's email address is available if they would just ask. Lots of us even have our emails listed in the email phone directory at switchboard.com. (Note: Check out www.switchboard.com.) How can a company be this far behind? Makes you wonder about their products and everything. If I were the planner, I'd find a different company...or maybe I should find a different planner who is more up-to-date.

Q: Well, I can't help you there. Tell me what else your dad liked about the Web TV bank rep he spoke with on TV?

they...have a live Web TV conference each week for their local clients to tune into

A: Oh, yeah, they invited my dad to an investment presentation with some big investment company. They say that they do that every quarter. He will love that! Who knows, I may go with him. He invited me. Oh, and they also have a live Web TV conference each month for their local clients to tune into. Kind of neat when you have an investment hour each month on the stuff that you own.

Q: What do you think that your financial planner would say if he knew that you were going with your dad to the investment presentation?

but this new relationship building on Web TV is just too convenient for people not to get involved with...

A: I think he would probably be upset. But Dad's right, he probably wouldn't even know. I wonder how he's doing now with the banks, CPAs and everyone doing the same thing. Plus, now with Web TV, gosh, Dad really likes that convenience. I do, too. Anyway, I hope that he is doing OK, but this new relationship building on Web TV is just too convenient for people not to get involved with it. Anyway, it's got to be hard for him.

Q: Why else do you sense that your agent might be having a hard time?

A: Well, selling an intangible product is pretty hard. I mean the products are all virtually the same with all companies. At least I can't see any difference. It's not like a car where you can see something that is visibly distinct, you know, something that you just have to have.

Q: But selling financial products was always an intangible sale. Why do you think that it's harder today?

A: Well, now that the banks and everyone else are contacting everyone directly, it's really got to be tough. Plus, now they offer these big investment events plus the Web TV monthly-reviews to keep you up-to-date. Did I tell you that a specialty "cruise only" travel company is cosponsoring this next investment event with a special presentation about the Greek Islands? That kind of grabs your attention and I could even get my wife to go to something like that even with the investment stuff - which she hates! It makes it more like an entertainment evening and not a seminar.

Q: Does your financial planner offer things like this?

A: My financial planner doesn't do anything like this. He is just a typical investment guy, I guess. He just sells stuff and about once a year he calls. Sometimes he calls on my Birthday, but even then he tries to get me to refer my friends to him. I don't like this constant request for names of my friends. It's not like we have a close relationship where I feel indebted and really want to help him. You can't have a close relationship when you see someone once a year. He is bad at staying in contact.

Q: Why do you think that he doesn't spend more time trying to do some unique events? I would think that his company would help him..

A: Well, speaking in his defense, I think he probably spends most of his time looking for a new customer. He's probably

> *I don't know why my planner didn't get involved with this new technology.*
>
> *...he shouldn't have waited.*

trying to survive. Maybe that's why he seems to focus on only asking me for a new name whenever I do see him. He's a nice guy but he doesn't do anything anymore unique than anyone else – at least not that I can determine. I know that if I were younger, and looking for someone to help me with financial issues, I would think twice about having a personal agent when I could get the convenience of the "instant Rep" on Web TV. This business has to be tough. I don't know why my planner didn't get involved with this new technology. Why didn't he do that? Do you think he just didn't see it coming? His company should have helped him, don't you think? But he shouldn't have waited. He just should have gotten involved somehow. What do you think? It's got to be tough.

The END

As a sales person, to remain indispensable to your clients in the future, it will be necessary to repackage your intangible product and recreate it into a "package of value," whose main characteristic is your consistent and unique visibility. Some refer to this as a tangible service product. The only way to accomplish this is by developing prospect familiarity through creative and repetitive events, unique contacts and unique services. Technology will be critical to this future strategy. Without the ability to

> *it will be necessary to take an intangible product and recreate it into a "package of value," whose main characteristic is its consistent visibility to the client and prospect. Some refer to this as a tangible service product.*

access your clients and prospects through the available communication technology, you won't be able to maintain your competitive advantage. The ability to interface with the customer on a personal basis through the Internet communication systems will be imperative.

Creating a Web site is not the solution for making you appear unique and distinct. It will not create an Identity Brand that differentiates you from the competition. Web sites may be necessary for providing client service, or for allowing clients a method to make instant changes to a flexible product, but a Web site will not create prospect attraction for the person who has never met you.

Only those representatives and offices that adopt Internet communication technology as a partner in their marketing strategies will thrive. You will need the ability and skills to display presale material to the client during a phone conversation on his or her computer screen or be able to forward it to their email with an agreement to call back later to discuss the information. A shared computer screen between two or more parties while conversing over the phone line will become the norm. All of these technologies are presently available. They will be widespread with your customers in the near future. Technology will integrate the TV, telephone and computer all into one package. It is going to happen fast.

The salespeople who survive in the future will not even be identifiable to their predecessors of yesterday. The personal sales representative will not be extinct, but success will require building direct relationships through entirely new communication systems. In many cases, your personal contact with a client or even a prospect will be through the interactive Internet or not at all. People, who want high-touch, personal relationships with their professionals will demand and expect alternatives to meeting with you. Time issues, business demands, privacy and conve-

your personal contact with a client or even a prospect will be through the interactive Internet or not at all

nience will require your ability to build personal relationships over the Internet. If you can't accommodate the way he or she wants to communicate, your client will leave for someone who can.

If you don't believe that technology will take a large piece of the market, remember that neither did anyone believe that selling sophisticated computers directly over the phone without a face-to-face salesperson could create a large company. Well just ask Dell® Computer, who generates millions in revenues on a daily basis how their strategy worked out. Now, what were your thoughts about financial service companies not being able to make much of an impact by going direct or clients not being receptive to interactive Web TV meetings?

If you believe that you can survive by essentially doing what you are doing now, you need to ask yourself what assumptions you are making that will need to hold true for that to happen. Then ask yourself, what would need to happen to make your assumptions invalid.

Technology and marketing may once have been viewed as strange bedfellows, no longer!

The bottom line is that you can't ignore technology if you are going to survive. You can't fight it and neither can you resist adapting. You must find the technology link to relationship marketing in the future or your business will languish, if not fail. Technology and marketing may once have been viewed as strange bedfellows, no longer! How will you begin to accumulate an email database, not just of clients but of desirable prospects?

How will you begin to accumulate an email database? What else will you do to stay abreast of the communication/technology opportunities?

Is Specializing Your Road to Success?

Eventually, as sales representatives become more capable at what they do, they struggle with the issue of whether to specialize. Dr. Thomas Stanley, author of *Networking with the Affluent,* says, "If I go back and look at the hundreds and hundreds of case studies that we have, what I find is that most of the extraordinary sales professionals in America who target the affluent are specialists." Most sales professionals who have continued to climb to new heights of success eventually came to a crossroad where they knew that they needed to narrow their focus. Once they took that step (if it were done correctly), they have come to realize that the change did not cause a loss; it caused a gain. As they narrowed their market, they broadened their appeal. Specializing enabled them to focus their marketing efforts to a more specific group of prospects. Not only did the prospect gain, but the sales professional gained a higher level of personal satisfaction. They gained new enthusiasm for what they did; their life's work took on new meaning. So, why don't more sales professionals take the plunge? What holds them back from doing what they know would be best for their careers?

As they narrowed their market, they broadened their appeal.

In the beginning stage of business, most new sales entrants sell to anyone whom they can get to listen. As their business and skills develop, they become more selective. Many feel that eventually as much as eighty percent of their original customer base become clients whose future needs require a skill that is well below their knowledge level. It causes an emotional struggle. Do I provide the service and consistent contact that I originally promised or do I eventually

if not dealt with, you will eventually become the senior agent who feels like a "de-fanged lion."

lose contact, which means my initial clients become abandoned or underserved? The answer is not as simple as some would lead you to believe. It is an emotional issue. If not dealt with, you will eventually become the senior agent who feels like a "de-fanged lion," always servicing past clients whose needs no longer challenge your intellect. You will constantly struggle with finding time to elevate your customer base. You know that you are capable of so much more, but there are no more hours in the day. You have no more time! There seems to be no way out. Your integrity won't allow you to abandon the clients that created your initial success. You have become a highly paid service clerk. You know that you have lost the vision and fulfillment in what you do. The price of continuing to ignore the direction of your current journey is too high, especially when there are strategies that can solve all of these issues.

Specialist vs. Generalist

Making the decision to become a specialist, is an acknowledgement that one can't or isn't willing to continue being all things to all people. It is a statement that he or she has decided to do what they do best and to do it more often. For most of these sales professionals, it was no small decision. It resolved an agonizing struggle. Having to decide what to "give up" and then imagining the potential impact or loss in income that could occur, even if only temporarily, was an emotional issue. Now they look back and wonder, "Why didn't I do it sooner?"

Becoming a "specialist"... resolved an agonizing struggle.

Now they...wonder, "Why didn't I do it sooner?"

The market segments that value specialization the most are twofold: 1) those who perceive their needs to be distinctly different from the masses and believe that they are really understood by only a few and 2) those who represent the wealthiest segment of society, who insist on specialized service providers and, usually, have no tolerance for nonperformance. Both of these groups will be more attracted to a specialist and will pay more for the assurance that they are working with a specialist than worry about price or quibble over whose product is "best." To them, the security in "knowing," though based on perception, that their provider is a specialist implies a distinct advantage and higher confidence level than the generalist can provide. Consequently, if the generalist becomes involved in competition with this segment, he or she will, more times than not, lose to the perceived specialist. Even the generalist who knows that he has a higher knowledge level and can help the client with a better solution will be at a disadvantage. He will normally lose.

When you are aiming for everyone, no one seems to come into focus very well.

The alternative to specializing is aiming for everyone. When you are aiming for everyone, no one seems to come into focus very well. As the saying goes, "When you try to appeal to everyone, you appeal to no one." Gerald R. Baron, author of *Friendship Marketing,* says, "Marketers instinctively understand you can't be all things to all people, but the traditional salesperson wants to argue with, 'Why not, if I can get the commission?' On the other hand, highly productive salespeople have a knack of determining very quickly how well both their skill level and their offerings match the customer's needs. If the match isn't there, they move on until they find that match."

Creating a Customer Service Enhancement

The first issue in deciding to specialize is deciding how to service the clients that no longer fit your market profile. There are numerous solutions to this issue. The first point is to realize that you are probably under servicing these people now. Even though you have a lot of files, don't let it create an illusion of security. You may be handling service requests, but proactive contact as well as profitability may be practically nonexistent. If these people could be handed over to a designated in-house customer service representative who could be introduced as an enhancement to your practice, the clients would perceive that you are growing and increasing service, even service to them! If the customer service representative could be introduced as their customer service representative, who then sent out periodic e-newsletters, e-birthday cards, yearly database questionnaires and handled personally requested changes, the client would actually increase their loyalty to you.

The job of the customer service representative would be to insulate you from contact. Even future product interest on the part of the client or a review request would be qualified to determine if your talent level justifies your involvement. If not, you could pass it on to a junior associate for a commission split. If the customer service representative were licensed, you could even negotiate a commission split on the case with him or her, assuming that he or she can handle it without

> *The job of the customer service representative... insulate you from contact.*

your involvement. If your office doesn't have a customer service representative, I would suggest creating one with other associates. Assign your block of business to the FULL-TIME customer service representative (not a part-time agent and part-time service rep – it doesn't work) and pay him a fifty-fifty split of your two percent service fees and twenty percent on additional sales that he uncovers on this block of business. You would be surprised how many sales a customer service representative can come up with when the incentive is motivating. It alleviates your service problems to a market that you have outgrown but keeps you in the loop for that "once-in-a-while surprise" when fortune prevails and one of your old clients does have a BIG opportunity for you to get involved in, if you only knew about it. Everyone wins and now you can focus your efforts on the top twenty percent of your client base. You've created a customer service enhancement for your existing client base, while being well on your way to establishing your new identity as a specialist.

The Benefit Is More Than Financial

Once you have dealt with the service issue for your existing client base, how can you be assured that "specializing" is your wisest decision? Narrowing your market and becoming a segment specialist always creates the highest level of customer appeal and corresponding income. It is no different than an orthopedic surgeon who attracts more people with sports injuries than a general doctor does. Who makes more money, the generalist who broadens his market more or the specialist who narrows his market further? Think about the brain surgeon! The narrower your market, the greater your appeal. Don't fool yourself. The road to success is not in increasing your product breadth. It is not in learning how to pick up all the loose change on the table. It is in your decision to narrow your focus and broaden your appeal.

becoming a segment specialist...creates the highest level of customer appeal

When shopping malls were first created, they were built around large department stores that were referred to as anchor tenants. Today's shopping malls are built around specialty stores. Which has more appeal, The Gap or Dillards? Victoria's Secret or J.C. Penney? If you could buy stock in Sears or Home Depot, which would you choose? It is said that if you want to gaze into the crystal ball to see how any industry is going to move into the future, just look at retail. Retail is said to always incur the first casualties when the buying patterns of the public begin to change. The consumer is demanding more specialties, not fewer. Unless you want to be a discounter, specializing is how retail will survive and how the most successful professionals will position themselves for the future.

It's Who You Are...Not What You Sell!

Theodore Levitt, in his book *The Marketing Imagination,* says that to successfully sell in the future will require "more and more intensified relationships." The consumer will be attracted by a view of personal distinction, not product. Your appeal will no longer rest on product needs. Appeal will be based on perception of "who you are," not "what you sell." The perception of "who you are" or your attractiveness to the prospect is not something that your company can do for you, nor does it have anything to do with the level of your company's national name recognition. "Brand is more than a name. It represents a relationship customers have come to know and value,"

> brand personality...attracts the client and...is created in the local market

says Regis McKenna, author of *Real Time.* A company's name recognition may help with credibility once a purchase decision is being made by the prospect but it is brand personality that attracts the client and brand personality is created in the local market. Theodore Levitt goes on to say that "Success goes to those who differentiate themselves [not their product] in ways that attract...superior numbers of customers to themselves." For the consumer, making a decision to grant an interview or to purchase a product is going to be far more dependent on impression than on fact and that impression is going to be locally dependent.

It will be you who will be responsible for creating a local market presence with a distinction, a brand essence that creates prospect appeal; a reputation that is visibly different and unique relative to the competition. After all, "specialists" who are truly specialists are capable of being identified by their "not yet clients," their prospects, not just their present clients. If your prospects can't identify your specialty, you don't have one. If your prospects can't identify your specialty, your specialty will perform poorly in meeting your income and business goals.

How Do I Choose a Specialty?

So, how do you create a distinction around you and your chosen specialty? First, decide what your personal strengths and interests are in the business. Chances are that they will be the same. Secondly, decide if your personal interest is measured more in the product category or a demographic category. A specialty does not have to be based on a core product or an advanced service. Not everyone has to become a small business specialist working with nonqualified plans. Neither do you have to base a specialty on a product focus such as disability income, investments or 401(k) retirement plans. A specialty can be just as effective by being based on a deep and genuine concern to serve a certain category of client. Imagine the identity that could be built if you operated under the name "Korean Only Financial" and limited your work to the Korean population of your city. Do you think that segment could be attracted to your focus? Would you have an easier task of focusing in on how to develop your reputation with this identified and "individualized" group? Lynn Upshaw says, in *Building Brand Identity*, "Smart brand marketers rethink who their targets are by acknowledging that they are not targets at all, but individual human beings." In other words, you may be able to create some brand positioning with a name, but you can't build brand personality with a general group. The group must be individualized in order to create consumer attraction, which is the result of creating a brand personality.

There is a firm in California run by Richard Metcalfe that operates under the name "Seniors Only Financial." It is well known, not only by their clients but by their prospects that they only work with clients over the age of fifty-five. Are they more expert than everyone else in this prospect market? Just ask the client. Better yet, get into competition with them over a prospect. You will more than likely lose before the competition even starts. Positioning has already been established. The name itself implies a higher level of expertise and specialty. The perception is well on its way to capturing the prospect's "mindshare." The brand personality is easy to target and Rick Metcalfe has done an incredible job. He knows who his prospects are and maintains a constant familiarization with them through all kinds of events and meaningful contacts. Some of his prospects have been influenced for months and even years before becoming clients. However, if you had asked them, even before they did business with Rick, who their specialist was, they would have answered... "Rick Metcalfe."

Harry Beckwith, author of *Selling the Invisible,* says, "Prospects do not buy how good you are at what you do. They buy how good you are at who you are." Metcalfe is truly one of the gurus of creating a "quality perception" in the prospect's mind, and he follows through with quality service. He knows that it's not just name recognition - not the company's and not his. Nor is what is promised or implied just smoke and mirrors. It takes substance, constant familiarization in unique ways, plus dedication to focus this narrowly and to become good at "who you are." Once successfully accomplished,

> *Harry Beckwith, author of Selling the Invisible, says, "Prospects do not buy how good you are at what you do. They buy how good you are at who you are."*

everyone feels good. The final result benefits everyone. Rick owns this market today and probably in the future. He has no anxiety about where his sales will come from in the future. He is Identity Branded as the specialist of choice not only to his clients but where it counts the most, to his prospects.

Creating an Automatic Advantage Over the Competition

What else can you do in order to increase your credibility as a specialist to your market segment? Most specialists would serve themselves well to create a "distinction identifier" that could help describe their positions to their market segments. This does not mean that you need a new business name or that you need to separate yourself from a large firm. Many, if not most, attorneys work under a firm name and still have distinct and recognizable specialties. A distinction identifier can be promoted to your market when conducting events, seminars and mailings. If possible, put it on your business card. In *Selling The Invisible*, Harry Beckwith, says, "If no prospect [notice that he does not say 'client'] can describe your position, you do not have one." A distinction identifier describes what you want your prospects to think. It is the initial qualifier that distinguishes you from your competitors. It usually implies an advantage. It is the initial impression that can go a long ways toward creating a perception of higher service, expertise and thus specialty...yours!

A distinction identifier...usually implies an advantage

Identifying the core message of your distinctiveness with a brief sentence or phrase can become a central theme of your uniqueness to your market segment. Identifiers can describe for whom a unique service is offered. It can be simple or clever, but it definitely needs to identify you from "the pack." It needs to have a unique appeal to your market. Examples of distinction identifiers are:

- "Business Owners Only. An Exclusive Focus. A Greater Expertise."
- "Integrated Financial Strategies - Reducing Taxes. Increasing Wealth."
- "The Million Dollar Estate Specialist. When Reducing Taxes Matters."
- "The $100,000 Investment Specialist. A Larger Commitment. A Bigger Outcome."
- "Korean Only Financial. When an Exclusive Focus Makes a Difference."

Harry Beckwith, in *Selling The Invisible,* says, distinction statements that are true to what you do "will make your word of mouth more effective. They can rally your troops [office colleagues]. They will get your marketing communications working as one." Decide on what your specialty focus is going to be and then create a distinction statement. Don't make it too general. Statements such as "Plan Now. Secure Your Future" are not distinctive, serve no purpose and add no attraction power for your market segment. It doesn't imply any advantage over the competition and says nothing about your "specialty." Be specific, not general. If it is done right, you will gain a competitive edge. Just make sure that you can now support your statement. Make sure that you can deliver what you are going to promise.

Don't Ruin Your Perceived Image

Once you have decided to proclaim a specialty, don't ruin your perceived image by violating your new position. If you have proclaimed that you specialize ONLY in nonqualified plans, when

...don't damage the market's perception of you as a specialist by once again looking like you "do it all."

asked if you handle group health insurance, the answer is NO. It is fine to answer that you have an associate who is a specialist at group health and ask permission for he or she to call them. Negotiate a split with the other specialist, but by all means, don't damage the market's perception of you as a specialist by once again looking like you "do it all." Don't even ask for the census information.

> You have to decide what it is that you no longer do and proclaim it as loudly as proclaiming your specialty.

The client's belief in your specialty will be greatly enhanced if you begin your dialogue by telling them what you don't do, what you are not a specialist in, what you have no clue about, before explaining what it is that you do specialize in. To illustrate this point, try telling someone, with no hint of humility, that your baseball-playing son is the number-one home run hitter in the state. They won't believe you! Now try telling someone that your son plays baseball and is the worst on his team at judging and catching fly balls; that he is fully capable of missing the simplest catches. However, he is the number-one home run hitter in the state. They will now believe you! People always believe what it is you have to say after you tell them what it is that you are not good at. That is one of the critical issues in becoming a specialist. You have to decide what it is that you no longer do and proclaim it as loudly as proclaiming your specialty. Become a "finder" for services no longer in your specialty and delegate those services accordingly. Don't lose your focus. Your clients will be unforgiving.

In conclusion, there are four elements in properly moving into a specialty focus. First, determine your area of expertise. Be realistic, but make a leap into the future. Second, determine how to delegate your service work and determine a way to totally insulate yourself from contacts that are below your skill level. A customer service representative could be a major help. Third, determine a market segment to which your specialty appeals and then "individualize" your market. You can't make an impression or capture "mindshare" from a general audience or from an entire community, but if you identify by name those whom you would like to have as prospects, you can now focus your marketing communication effectively. You can create a brand personality. Remember that if your prospects (not clients) cannot describe your specialty, you don't have one. Fourth, create a visibility plan. How will you clearly communicate your specialty? How will you continually familiarize yourself to your market? What will you do to surprise the prospect and to look unique when compared to your competition? The future belongs not to those who have all the answers but to those who have a distinction. How will you, over time, successfully provide an answer to the prospect's question of "Why you?" before they have even had a face-to-face interview with YOU…the specialist.

The more alike an industry becomes, the more important a local distinction becomes. If you are distinct enough and continually visible to your market segment, even your nonclients (your prospects) will regard you as the mark of excellence in your field. Your job is to raise awareness and create a distinction, a brand personality.

Identity Branding is and will become as important a prerequisite to gaining prospect access in the future as a poker chip is necessary for entering a poker game. It doesn't guarantee success, but without it you will not even have a chance to play. Declaring a specialty can help create favoritism. It can give you a competitive edge. It can also rekindle your spark and enthusiasm for your career.

Write out what ideas you can adapt to narrow your focus and broaden your appeal to your market segment.

Little Items Can Build Brand Loyalty...or NOT

A critical issue for surviving the future is whether you can provide positive experiences to the prospects or clients in the way that they want them provided. The ways that they want them to be provided are changing quickly. There are two criteria here to consider. One of the criteria is "positive" and the other is "in the way that they want it." The evaluation of those conditions comes from the client or prospect, not from you.

If the client or prospect is not happy with how they are getting what they want, no explanation is going to build, sustain or enhance your Identity Brand. The perception of who you are and your differentiation to the competition is going to be

Once a good perception is created, the consumer's mind closes to new input that would allow for reconsideration, a major factor in brand loyalty.

irrevocably harmed. No one is going to care about your explanations about why they can't get what they want in the way that they want it. Once a negative perception is created, it is virtually impossible to change. However, the good news is that the opposite is also true. Once a good perception is created, the consumer's mind closes to new input that would allow for reconsideration, a major factor in brand loyalty.

If you regularly drink COKE® you don't care that you chose Pepsi® in the taste test at the supermarket. When they inform

Preference is always based on perception over fact.

you of your taste choice and hand you the half-price Pepsi coupon, sometime during your shopping excursion you will ignore the results, negate the explanations, not care about the price advantage and slide another twelve pack of COKE into your shopping basket. The facts don't matter. "Don't bother me with the facts! My mind is made up. I like COKE!"The lesson is to make sure that your prospects form positive perceptions of you very quickly. Preference is always based on perception over fact.

Lynn Upshaw, author of *Building Brand Identity,* says, "Brands have no right to exist." Brands are usually not created nor justified due to superior product. However, brands dominate product choice in our society. Brands account for over ninety percent of all products purchased in America. Brand dominance begins when the consumer is provided with experiences, which create impressions and result in capturing "mindshare." Brands stay dominant by maintaining consistent familiarity with positive experiences. People rely on only partial facts and initial impressions to make their initial judgments. Once judgments are made and brand preference is established, people rarely change their minds. Inadequate time, patience and lack of expertise usually discourages reconsideration, even when new facts are presented. It takes effort and emotion to make a decision. Even if imperfect, a decision helps to simplify the person's life. To reconsider other facts, which would challenge their initial decision, would require that they "recomplicate" their lives with more effort and more emotional stress. Why? They were comfortable with their initial decision.

Have you ever heard someone say, "Don't confuse me with the facts. My mind is made up." Brands provide the easiest way for consumers to simplify their lives in an information overloaded society. As long as consistent familiarization continues, in a way that pleases them, the consumer has no reason to change. Loyalty is established! Hopefully, their loyalty is connected to your Identity Brand.

Maintaining loyalty requires consistent familiarization. It also requires constantly asking yourself if there is any thing that you are doing, or not doing, that the consumer wishes you would change. For instance, how many of your clients or prospects would prefer having you communicate with them via the Internet versus receiving another printed mailing? Do you know the answer? A database questionnaire sent periodically to your clients would provide that type of information. With the daily barrage of junk-mail, this is no small matter for many consumers. How many people in your market segment wish that you would stop sending a printed newsletter and, instead, send them the newsletter by email? If you can't do that now, you either have the wrong newsletter or the wrong technology, because both are currently available. If you aren't moving from print to technology, some of your clients and prospects, especially business owners and technology proficient individuals - often higher-income people - will be less than appreciative in the near future.

Not knowing what the client wants or not providing what the client wants in the way that he or she want it is far more critical today than at any other time in history. Clients expect what they want in the way they want it and they expect you to be responsive and current in meeting their expectations. Research and experience shows that the majority of your prospects would prefer having newsletters sent by email instead of through the regular mail. Are you listening and responding? You need to know what your clients want. It will eventually make an impact to building or sustaining your personal brand loyalty...positively or negatively.

E-Relationship™...Are You Current?

How many times have you had a prospect say "no" to your request for an appointment? You really want to see this prospect or client but you have run into the proverbial brick wall. Sure, there are times when you no matter what you try, you can't get the appointment, but that doesn't mean you should disappear and then call back in twelve months expecting that something magical has happened to your prospects willingness to accept your appointment request. If you include them as part of your structured branding plan, focusing on consistent familiarization over the next twelve months, you can expect good future results. This familiarization can be achieved through newsletters (consider an email version), invitations to consistent unique events and even casual personal contacts that will naturally occur through your market segment interaction. However, before giving up on your phone request for an initial meeting, why not ask permission to send occasional E-Relationship™ Financial e-Storyboards (www.e-relationship.com), accentuating the type of work that you do. Tell them that they can request additional details if a particular subject triggers their interest, and that you will check back in a few months to see if you could grab a casual lunch. You will always get an affirmative response, allowing you to continue building a compelling attraction with your prospect.

E-Relationship Financial Storyboards provide the prospect with basic, but brief, educational information on the unwanted financial consequences of not having a buy-sell, a supplemental deferred compensation plan for the business owner, a 401(k) plan for the employees, an estate plan to eliminate devastating financial losses, strategic ideas for reducing taxes, and over seventy other financial subjects you can choose from. E-Relationship Storyboards are problem focused, not solution focused. They provide the prospect value by providing an educational glimpse of the problem, not an intellectual description of the solution.

> *E-Relationship...provide the prospect value by providing an educational glimpse of the problem, not an intellectual description of the solution.*

Prospects are hesitant about granting appointments when they lack information about what you do or the problems you address when they have no evidence of the sales professional's likability, trustworthiness or competency. If the prospect or client will give you permission, send occasional e-Financial Storyboards about different ideas. Instead of having to accept a "no" to your appointment request, this strategy keeps the door open, allows you to provide value and gives you permission to call the prospect back. Hopefully, during the next contact, the prospect will be more receptive to your appointment request. After all, you will have increased your uniqueness, your professionalism and their knowledge.

You may decide that, depending upon the circumstances, a two-phone call approach is a better way to make many of your initial appointment requests to certain prospects, such as business owners or more affluent individuals, and not just a way to salvage an initial rejection. This new way to make a phone call would be to introduce yourself, to inform them that you are not going to ask for an appointment but that you would like their permission to email occasional financial information about an issue that may be of interest to them. After they have a few days to review it, you could suggest calling back to see if a casual lunch might be appropriate. Sound too radical, this two-phone call approach? So did going from a one-interview sales approach to a two-interview sales approach in the 1970s.

Today's consumer is more skeptical than at any other time in history. Before the consumer feels comfortable developing a business relationship, one's trust needs to have been established. There is no better way to initiate a trust relationship than to provide value to a prospect before a contact is made. Providing the prospect with educational information is providing "value." It demonstrates, even from your initial contact, that your focus is on "giving" and not just "getting."

E-Financial Storyboards (www.e-relationship.com) will differentiate you from the competition; certainly the strategy will be unique and distinct. Pushing financial information out to the prospect has a significant advantage over encouraging prospects to go into your Web site. You are notified when the prospect opens an e-Financial Storyboard. You don't know if they ever visit your Web site. If the prospects are technologically proficient, the chance of them reviewing your material is greater than if it were a printed brochure sent through the US Mail. Recent research shows that electronic mail is over 300% more effective in conveying a message than material sent through US Mail. E-Relationship Storyboards are more contemporary, distinct and controlled than directing a prospect to a Web site. Check out: www.e-relationship.com. Ask yourself: am I still communicating the way I always have, or can I deliver what the client or prospect wants in the way that they want it? If not, you will eventually notice the consequences.

Technology is always evolving. It is no longer in opposition to relationship building. It is a relationship enhancer. You must keep current with how technology can provide better ways for communicating with your prospects. In the world of the new "Darwinian" technology, only the fastest will survive. Don't get left behind.

Here is a copy of an
E-Relationship Financial Storyboard™ on
Taxes – Small Business Owner

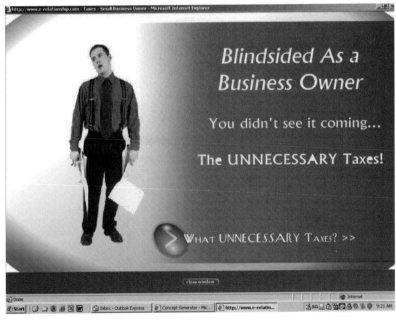

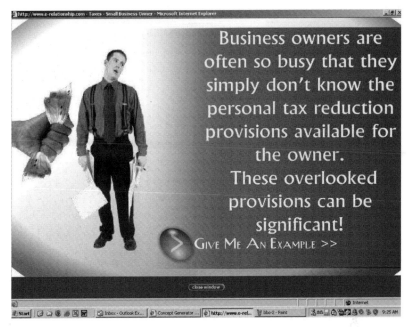

Business owners are often so busy that they simply don't know the personal tax reduction provisions available for the owner. These overlooked provisions can be significant!

GIVE ME AN EXAMPLE >>

© 2004 Identity Branding, Inc.

Robert E. Krumroy

Here is a copy of an
E-Relationship Financial Storyboard™ on
Taxes: The Growth Killer

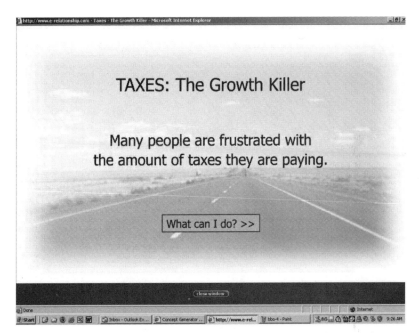

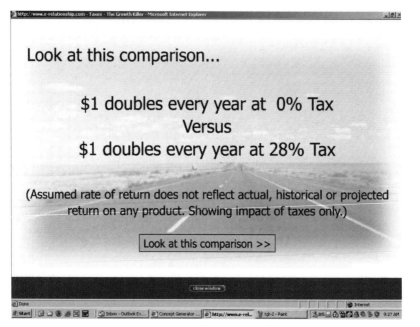

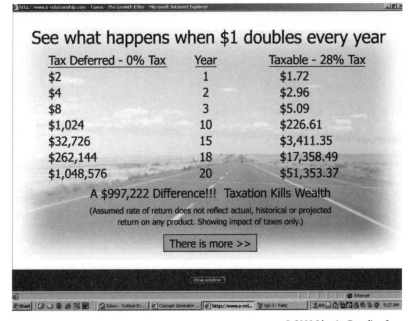

See what happens when $1 doubles every year

Tax Deferred - 0% Tax	Year	Taxable - 28% Tax
$2	1	$1.72
$4	2	$2.96
$8	3	$5.09
$1,024	10	$226.61
$32,726	15	$3,411.35
$262,144	18	$17,358.49
$1,048,576	20	$51,353.37

A $997,222 Difference!!! Taxation Kills Wealth

(Assumed rate of return does not reflect actual, historical or projected
return on any product. Showing impact of taxes only.)

There is more >>

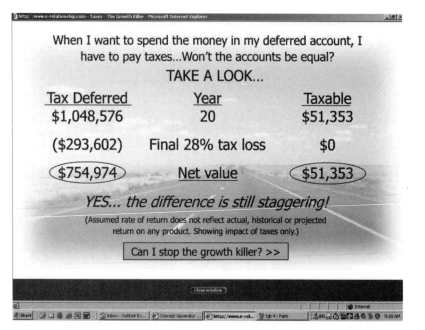

When I want to spend the money in my deferred account, I
have to pay taxes...Won't the accounts be equal?

TAKE A LOOK...

Tax Deferred	Year	Taxable
$1,048,576	20	$51,353
($293,602)	Final 28% tax loss	$0
$754,974	Net value	$51,353

YES... the difference is still staggering!

(Assumed rate of return does not reflect actual, historical or projected
return on any product. Showing impact of taxes only.)

Can I stop the growth killer? >>

© 2000 Identity Branding, Inc.

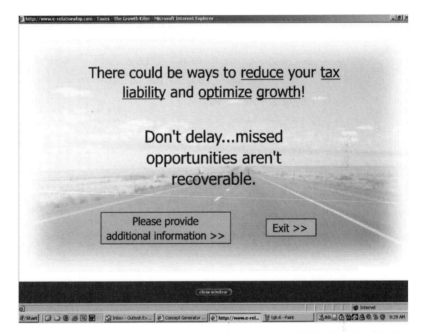

What communication technology should I be utilizing to enhance my relationship with my prospects and clients. (i.e., e-newsletters, e-Relationship Financial Storyboards, etc)

Brochures – Necessary or Not?

Most local marketing in the financial services industry is poorly done. It has consisted primarily of distributing company and product brochures, a few local agents doing some occasional print advertisements and, in the last few years, a little training on target market identification. Why has marketing been so overlooked? Because, for years, marketing didn't have to be done. There were plenty of easy-to-access prospects. Selling and prospecting were the whole game...but no longer. Attraction marketing must become your new business platform if you are going to survive. You must create an annual prospect attraction plan that should be the lifeblood of your business, your yearly roadmap that directs all of your actions.

There are over one million financial advisors in the United States. Guess what? Most of them have the same brochures that you do. Only the covers are different. Your job in the new marketing environment is to create a brand personality that truly stands apart, is unique, distinct and differentiated from the competition. Marketing is getting the consumer to notice you first! It is achieved by doing things differently. It is not achieved by getting them to notice that you do what everyone else does, even if you can prove that you do it a little better.

Your job is to create "likability"... We trust people whom we like.

Brochures can play a role in validating what you say you do, but they are not a factor in building your brand personality or in attracting prospects. Brochures should never be used as mass mailing pieces to prospects that have never heard of you. Remember the *Prospect Fishbowl?* Where is your individualized list of future prospects (at least five hundred) within your market segment? If you don't have that complete, developing one is the first priority! Do you want to make your first impact at your first

137

face-to-face encounter with the prospect, or before then? How much better would your results be if one thousand prospects noticed you and created an attraction for you before they ever met you? Would your sales soar? Sure they would. People buy you - not product and not your brochure! People give interviews most easily to people they like. Your job is to create "likability" for yourself and to create a constant familiarization. We trust people whom we like and our liking is magnified when we discover a social or belief connection. These are the greatest elements that create the strongest and most lasting perception.

So, where do brochures fit in? If you are going to have one, brochures need to be personalized to you instead of to your company. Most traditional brochures promote nothing distinct. They promote product and services through an array of bullet points. An effective brochure should promote your personal differentiation and likability, not product. It should accentuate your community social connection or belief commonality to the prospect. It is only when you know your market segment as individuals that you can put together a personal brochure that talks about your specialty and how you personally relate to the market. Specialization elevates value perception. A narrower focus attracts greater appeal. The brochure that can visibly show your "likability" and differentiation to a specific market segment can add credibility to your image.

How often have you gotten excited about a brochure you received from a financial company? Are yours just like those? Attraction marketing is about creativity and innovation, not imitation. If you are going to use a brochure, have one created personally for you. Get out of your boring business suit and away from the desk. Put on your shorts. Take the spouse, children and the dog for a family picture in front of a boat at the local lake. Have the picture taken while putting a life jacket on your child and caption the picture on your brochure with the words, "When You Want an Advisor Who Is Committed to Great Performance,

But Never Loses Focus on Safety." Now, write about your commitment to performance, family and security. Make the brochure a humanizing touch point with which your market can identify. Are you getting the idea? Take a picture while wearing your jogging or tennis outfit, coaching a children's sporting team, being involved at Habitat for Humanity, participating in a community board, teaching a class and relate your personal beliefs about being part of a team or your winning attitude toward life as elements that you incorporate when working with clients. Look real! Be likeable! Reveal who you are personally, and relate how it applies to your business. Make your brochure distinctly different and unique from anything you have ever seen. Let it be a differentiator, not another boring imitation.

Write any ideas that you may have about creating a brochure that would have personal appeal to the values of your identified market segment.

Producing a Radio Talk Show Program and Becoming a Local Celebrity

We have already discussed why traditional print advertising is the single greatest waste of money that most agents and financial advisors ever spend. Radio advertising is, also, at the top of that "waste-of-money" list. First of all, it is expensive. Therefore, it doesn't get done with much regularity, but even if it did, it rarely focuses on a cohesive market segment. Secondly, the station programming may focus on a specific age bracket of listeners, but this is hardly a criterion for market segmentation or individualization. However, radio is one area that may provide an exception to the rule for those who have the talent and desire to pursue the following opportunity.

Radio is still a medium that can create local celebrity status in a very short period of time, if you have the ability and personality to communicate over the airwaves in a talk show format. We have helped financial advisors produce numerous radio talk shows that are still on the air today. These "everyday" advisors are now celebrities within their communities. Not a week passes without someone commenting to them about their radio talk shows. Listeners believe that these advisors are superior to others in their field. Even prospects who don't listen to the show but are given an audio CD (which cost less than one-dollar to produce – including the plastic case) titled, "The Ten Most Frequently Asked Financial Questions," immediately conclude that the advisors must be more advanced and therefore preferable to their competition.

These financial advisors have created consumer attraction and preference through radio talk shows. Financial radio talk shows are, and will continue to be, in high demand. The radio talk show celebrities can easily accumulate large *Prospect Fishbowls* of names by offering to include the listener on their occasional financial email communication. Simply telling the listeners to call a voicemail phone number to leave their name, email address and phone number (optional) will generate hundreds of signups over a few short months. Encouraging listeners to call in to request personal meetings will result in at least four to eight calls per week. Being a celebrity on a weekly or daily radio program creates an impact before the prospect has met you. This is marketing, not because of radio ads but because of the visibility, the uniqueness and the differentiation of YOU within the market place. The audio CDs that

financial advisors... created consumer attraction and preference through radio talk shows

you can have produced for one-dollar are far less expensive and more effective than other alternatives in the industry. They are not self-promoting. They are recordings of actual financial questions and answers that help build a quality perception for the consumer and defines "why you." This is a far more convincing promotional piece for differentiating you than a generic brochure or a self-promotional audiotape.

There are two ways to produce an effective radio show. One is to find a local talk show station (usually an AM station) and explore its interest in having a financial call-in show. The show should last for one hour. Don't be surprised if they expand it to one and one-half hours in the near future. Talk time around commercials is approximately seventeen minutes during every thirty minutes of airtime. You can answer three questions per half-hour. You should broadcast during the weekday, not on weekends. Afternoon drive time starting around 3:00 p.m. is ideal. The local cellular telephone companies will assign a courtesy speed dial option (one number plus *) for drivers calling in during broadcast time if you will promote the cellular company and the number. You can announce this during the broadcast. It just adds more credibility to your new celebrity status.

Selling advertising spots produces the largest portion of a radio station's income and our financial shows were rated close, if not second, to Rush Limbaugh in popularity. Now, I will not comment on whether I am a Rush Limbaugh fan, but I did like the comparative ratings. The station made a lot of money by having a no-cost, popular show of this magnitude, which they could load with advertisements. Everyone was happy: the station, the advertisers, the listeners and the "celebrity" financial advisors. You should be able to convince the station to let you do the show for free for at least four to twelve weeks while they measure its popularity. If they charge you a nominal fee, the agreement should be renegotiated to even less, or nothing, after the first quarter as the show becomes popular, and it will. Get an audio CD of a financial talk show from a radio program broadcast somewhere in the United States, give it to the station and discuss the benefits of producing a similar program. Financial programs are popular with listeners and both you and the station will be pleased with the results.

You should be able to convince the station to let you do the show for free...

As you are getting established, you may have to ask friends, clients and business associates to call in questions for approximately three weeks. Make sure their questions are related to wealth, retirement and financial investment issues and not insurance. You can develop a list of good questions such as, "How do I best diversify my 401(k) plan at work and is it OK to put most of my contribution into my own company's stock? It has really been performing well and it is one of my options." You may need to have a "theme" to talk about for the first few weeks as the show gets off the ground. Make sure the theme is investment based and not insurance based. The public regards insurance, even equity based variable life, as an

They want to hear about "WEALTH, INVESTMENT, RETIREMENT and PROFIT" issues.

expense. Disability income and long-term care insurance are also regarded as expenses. NO ONE wants more expenses and listeners are not interested in listening to a talk show program based on expense items. If you want to reach the senior audience, talk about elder care or identity theft, not insurance products. They will stay tuned when your broadcast focuses on quality of life issues, wealth, investment and retirement strategies.

It is unlikely that you will ever receive a call-in question about insurance. That should tell you something. Although you will have lots of opportunities to sell a lot of life and disability insurance in planning interviews with people who call-in to meet with you, it is not what you use to attract attention or to gather a listener-base over the airwaves. Very soon, you will have plenty of calls coming into your talk show and their questions will all be on investment issues. Talking about tax issues are also good if you get a lull in call-ins. Annuities are good subject matter, but be ready when someone calls to challenge you on the justification of the

The more specific your answers are, the better your ratings will be...

inside mortality and management expenses versus a mutual fund and the long-term taxable gain advantage. The more specific your answers are, the better your ratings will be and the more call-ins you will get.

Your compliance department will need to be notified that you have a call-in-radio show. They are fully aware that there is nothing you can do to prepare, and nothing in advance that you can send for their compliance review. This does not mean that meeting compliance standards when answering questions from your listeners is not your responsibility. It is. It should go without saying that you can't guarantee returns or make projections. Know the rules.

One of the greatest fears about being on radio is not knowing an answer to a question. You don't have to worry about not knowing an answer or having someone call to harass you. The radio station has a screener who answers the calls and then asks what the caller's question is. The screener will then type the question on a prompter-screen in front of you so that you know who is on hold and to what the question pertains. You will probably want to have some research material and computer support with you. If you don't know the answer, instruct your screener to tell the caller that you have other people on hold, get the caller's number and ask to call him or her back personally. Once your show develops a following, you will have numerous callers backed up. Select the questions you know that you can handle the best and answer those on the air.

A great suggestion is to produce the show in partnership with another financial advisor in your firm, or have an administrative assistant present that can access research information on the computer for the next question while you are answering the current question. Our most popular shows had two financial advisor personalities. Don't bring in other professionals more than once a month to share the show, such as attorneys or CPAs. The show needs to promote YOU, not an outside attorney or CPA. Using two financial advisors does

Very quickly you will create "likability"; "likability" is the most important initial element for developing trust in a relationship.

have one advantage in that you will quickly learn how to play off of each other. When one of you knows the answer better than the other, it is an easy hand-off to that person. Plus, you can make fun of each other; you can be self-deprecating and feel the audience laugh with you. Very quickly you will create "likability." likability is the most important initial element for developing trust with your prospects and even your listening audience.

Producing a Three-Minute Daily Broadcast Radio Show

Instead of doing a live talk show, consider producing a three-minute broadcast or vignette to be aired at the same time every day, Monday through Friday. The first one that I originally helped launch is still running today. It is called *"Managing Money Based On God's Principles,"* a Christian financial show. Two financial professionals record two weeks' worth of vignettes (ten "three-minute" programs) every other week. This takes a maximum of ninety minutes and the radio station runs them at 7:45 a.m. every weekday. The recording is always done at the radio station, therefore, you incur no outside recording expense. Once you have accumulated sixty good vignettes, you can rotate the same material every three months. Make minor changes to the existing ones and record a few new ones when appropriate to keep the series contemporary. Because these are prerecorded spots, they do need to be sent to your compliance department for approval. Again, make sure that all the subjects are financial and investment related. You can test insurance-related topics for yourself. It will be quickly evident that the program produces no calls that day.

This show is broadcast on a fundamental Christian radio station and yields ten to eighteen call-ins per week. Within twelve months, the financial advisors created a *Prospect Fishbowl* of over one thousand call-in names by offering their free e-newsletter.

> *...the financial advisors created a Prospect Fishbowl of over one thousand call-in names by offering their free newsletter.*

This station has a cohesive group of listeners, who share a deep religious belief, which is an anomaly to most secular stations. As a cohesive market segment that was now identified with individual names in the advisors' database, the two advisors initiated their first annual prayer breakfast, which brought in over two hundred people. The advisors' exposure through radio produced continual invitations

They were having an impact on prospects before they met them...

to speak at local events. They became widely known in the Christian community as celebrities, and became actively involved in the city's Christian Business Expo and a number of other business and social opportunities, which were centered on their faith. Each quarter, they put together an investment seminar based on biblical principles, announced them on radio and through e-invitations. They put together an audio CD of their "Ten Most Requested Financial Topics," which they handed out enthusiastically. The audio CD proved to be significantly more meaningful than a simple business card when they met with new prospects and existing clients. They also used their audio CD as an "interest hook" when requesting an initial appointment by offering to bring a free copy with them when they met the prospect... GET THE IDEA? They were becoming a little bit famous, Identity Branded to a specific market segment. They were having an impact on prospects before they met them, rather than waiting until their first face-to-face encounter. They were getting the prospect to notice them first in a market segment where they themselves were emotionally committed to a belief commonality. **This is marketing at its best!**

The following script is typical of their three-minute vignettes

Opening the broadcast – *the program's theme music is playing*

DJ Opens: *"It's time for our daily broadcast, "Managing Money Based On God's Principles," with your hosts Brad Smith and Kevin Hanner. If you have a financial question you would like answered, give us a call on our toll free number at 1-800-000-0000. Here are Brad and Kevin, professionals and registered representatives with (broker dealer) in (city) with today's question (or strategy)."*

Brad: *(reads question or announces the theme)* *"We have a question from a listener today that reads, 'I have been in my company's 401(k) plan for a number of years now but don't know if I am investing in the right funds to get the best return. Everyone seems to have an opinion but isn't there some kind of practical formula or advice you can give us?'"*

Kevin: *"Many listeners have expressed to us their frustration with not knowing how their 401(k) works and how they can maximize their benefits from it."*

Brad: *"That is true. And a lot of times people who feel this way end up frustrated or too embarrassed to ask questions or, worse yet, they hold back on how much they contribute to their retirement plan."*

Kevin: *"You know, Brad, a recent Wall Street Journal article said that most people do not understand their 401(k) plan and that they end up investing poorly and then miss out on the biggest gains. It's not just an occasional occurrence. It happens all the time."*

Brad: *"Another one of our listeners about a month ago called from the city of Thomasville and expressed the same concern. The good news was that she was contributing to her 401(k) plan and had done well, but it wasn't diversified. She was just never really comfortable with not having any defined strategy...it made her nervous."*

Kevin: *"I remember, Brad, she was mostly invested in her own company's stock with about twenty-five percent in another option. Although it had done well, her company's stock was trending down and the other option she had chosen didn't look promising for the next twelve months. As we spoke for a while, she realized that she had no investment strategy, no yearly rebalancing strategy and very little diversification."*

Brad: *"You know, Kevin, we provided information that helped her create a professional investment strategy that was more appropriate for her age and guided her into diversifying her account among four investment options within her plan. Now she doesn't have to worry about the account every day and she knows how to rebalance her account every twelve months for safety and to hopefully get the best return."*

Kevin: *"You know, Brad, in the Bible, God talks a lot about the importance of gaining wisdom and understanding. In Proverbs 4:6 it says, 'Do not forsake wisdom and she will protect you.' I think that applies to all areas of our lives."*

Brad: *"You're right, Kevin. Listeners...don't ignore your 401(k) plan or try to guess at how you should be investing. Your mistakes could cost you the retirement that you have dreamed about. If you would like an information packet on the best strategies for investing* *in your 401(k) plan, please call us at 1-800-000-0000. Don't delay. The information packet is FREE...just call."*

DJ closes: *(theme music starts to play) "If you would like the information packet on today's topic or if you have a question related to finances or money, please call our number at 1-800-000-0000. And be sure to join Brad and Kevin tomorrow morning here at (station) for the daily broadcast of 'Managing Money Based on God's Principles.'"*

This script is an example of a one-minute secular broadcast

Opening the broadcast – *Theme music playing from the song "MONEY"*

DJ opens: *"Your future financial success is a matter of money and strategy. So with answers to your daily questions, here is (name), your professional here in (city), registered representative with (XXXXXXXXXXXX) and host of your 7:45 a.m. daily broadcast, 'The One-Minute Financial Strategy.'"*

Financial professional (YOU!): *"Retirement planning is a critical issue for women. Did you know that, according to the National Center for Women and Retirement Research, 85% of all women will die alone either because of being widowed, divorced, or never having married."*

"73% of retired women have no retirement plan and the AARP reports that of the 12% of all elderly people living in poverty, 74% of them are women."

"If you're a woman, you have an 80%-90% chance that someday you will be solely responsible for your own finances. You can't afford to be uninformed about investing and finances."

"If you would like our FREE booklet entitled 'Empowering Financial Information for Women,' call us at _____. Again that number is _____."

DJ closes: *(theme music starts playing) "Don't delay. Requesting additional information is free. Our daily financial broadcast may last only one minute, but your* *future will last a lifetime. That phone number for the free information is _____."*

> If producing a radio program has created an interest, write down the station that comes to your mind, the type of program (talk or prerecorded) that appeals to you and any other issues that may apply. Just write down your thoughts and see what happens.

"Managing Money Based on God's Principles"

The New **94.1** WWGL "Today's Best Christian Music"

**Kevin Hanner & Brad Smith
can be heard each morning
at 7:45 am on WWGL and
can be contacted at (336) 852-8650.**

"The plans of the diligent lead to profit."
Proverbs 5:5

"Creating Simple and Unique Solutions to Complex Issues"

"Your Money Matters"

600 WSJS

John Hardy and Gib McEachran can be heard
every Wednesday from 3:30 to 5:00 pm on WSJS
and contacted daily at (336) 852-8650

"Every man is the architect of his own fortune."
- Sallust

Build A Well-Structured Branding Plan

If you are an agency manager, it is neither necessary nor practical to focus your entire agency on a single targeted group. Much like a law firm, however, you do need to help each associate find a unique focus in which they can become deeply and emotionally involved. Help them to individually construct a well-structured branding and prospect attraction plan and then commit to managing it with them. Guy Kawasaki, author of *Selling the Dream*, says, "The obvious benefit of a plan is that it serves as the guiding light...In addition, writing a plan forces you to think critically, to better understand your cause, and to communicate with others in the organization." The more complete the plan, the better your communication will be and the better the support you can extend, particularly to your more established sales professionals.

If your sales associates are not willing to go out of their way to get involved with the market segment(s) that they are considering as a focus, this prospect group is not for them. If they want to defend their marketing problems solely as either lack of product or advanced knowledge needs, start looking for their replacements. Regardless of their seniority or their past success, they won't reach their full potential in this new environment, unless they have an attraction marketing plan. Without an attraction marketing plan, the chances are they won't even survive.

Working harder...will not substitute as a solution to market access problems.

Working harder will eventually not overcome the loss in income that a worsening market-access problem will incur. Being coached to get better organized, to become more efficient and to become a better delegator, though all worthy goals, will not substitute as a solution to market-access problems. You must meet the new marketing expectations of the consumer in order to survive. You must become a "package of value," which is far more significant than the product you sell or your promise to provide good service. Dr. Thomas Stanley, in *Networking With the Affluent,* sums it up thusly, "Sales and marketing professionals focusing on their own needs, their own products, their own services, their own fees and commissions, and not on those of their targets, will not be successful in this arena." Regarding the needs of your target markets, they must be able to describe your differentiation, distinction and uniqueness relative to the competition. They must be able to answer the question, "Why you?" Answering that question by creating consumer preference and "mindshare" in an individualized market can only be accomplished from becoming...

DISTINCT, and if not...EXTINCT!

How to Get Started

IDENTITY BRANDING

Robert E. Krumroy

Becoming Unique and Distinct

Building an Identity Brand is more than a strategic planning process; it's an active relationship process. Regis McKenna, author of *Real Time*, says, "Brand is an active experience." It therefore requires a structured plan for consistent review as to progress and accountability to your strategy. You must create a perception of uniqueness relative to the competition. The

> *Building an Identity Brand is...an active relationship process...*

prospect is incapable of judging expertise, service promises or even product superiority, but they can judge whether they are attracted to your brand personality. You can't do the same things as the competition and expect to increase prospect attraction. Neither should you focus on taking away a portion of market share from your competitor. You must focus on owning the entire market segment. You must create a solid basis of differentiation that captures prospect "mindshare," makes constant impressions and creates a distinctive perception that you offer a higher quality "package of value." By becoming unique and distinct, you will be the recipient of many benefits.

The Six Benefits of Identity Branding YOU

James R. Gregory and Jack G. Wiechmann, authors of *Marketing Corporate Image*, say, "Branding is a declaration of who we are, what we believe and why you should put your faith in [us] our company." In today's market, the expanding breadth of products, everyone's claims of superiority and the intrusive marketing methods used in an attempt to sell them, bewilder the consumer. Roman G. Hiebing, Jr. and Scott W. Cooper, authors of *The One-*

159

Day Marketing Plan, say, "...the consumer does not have the time or energy to know everything necessary to make the right choice." They are frustrated in today's advertising and product proliferation environment. There is simply too much product noise in the market place. Consumers want to simplify their life choices. They are becoming far more concerned with making a decision on "whom to believe" than they are in determining "what to believe." That is why branding has become such a focus for tangible products. Once the brand is in the consumer's mind, everything else becomes much less of a concern. Branding YOU as the product of choice brings with it the same benefit as branding a tangible product. These are the six specific benefits you can expect:

1. Easier and perpetual access to prospects who trust you

2. Faster acceptance and implied trust by new prospects referred to you in complementary markets

3. Shortened sales cycle

4. Larger average sales

5. Maintaining a defined focus is easier

6. Stronger client and organizational loyalty

Once you have completed the decision as to the market(s) segment you are going to focus your branding efforts, you will begin to see an almost immediate improvement in market access to your prospects. You will see an easier and a perpetual access open up to your prospects, what I refer to as the benefit of building a prospect highway. It

You will see...perpetual access open up to your prospects...a prospect highway.

can be argued as to whether the change is internal (psychological) or external but, regardless of the nature of the change, it is real. You will begin to view your market with ownership. You will begin to think in terms of "giving" and not "getting." It is now YOUR valuable asset whose future growth is in your hands. Once you begin to implement your branding plan of "familiarity and distinction," you will begin to see the market access door open to your requests to introduce your services to the new prospect.

As your career continues to develop, you will always have opportunities for expanding or refocusing your market in line with your skill level. The biggest mistake that most sales professionals make is working with people who are below their skill level. Once you have determined your ideal profile of a prospect, don't violate it. Remember the days when you scraped, clawed and fought your way to any sale that you could get your hands on? Don't you wish now that you would have focused your efforts more? Think of all the time you wasted on all of those prospects who looked so promising but never worked out. Well, don't regress. It's easy, but detrimental to find yourself chasing a sale that you have no business pursuing. Guy E. Baker, CLU, MSFS, one of the leading producers in the insurance industry and Top of the Table since 1977, says in his book *Why People Buy,* "I still find it hard to say 'no' to a potential prospect. I have had to discipline myself to only focus on the 'profile' prospects. I want to talk to people who are going to enhance my long-term business objectives. If there is no rational reason to accept a case that is outside my business plan, then I need to walk away."

As your personal market reputation develops, your existing market segment will provide opportunities for you to be introduced to new markets and prospects that fit your prospect profile equally as well. If you have positioned yourself effectively in your initial market segment, you will have faster market acceptance to these new prospects because of your reputation and the "lead in" that you will naturally receive. Once your branding plan is structured, you will find it easy to expand to include these new prospects and to make a similar impact on them as you have on your initial market segment.

The selling sales cycle within your market segment will also become more efficient the greater your personal Identity Brand becomes. You will also see your average sales size increase. This would not have happened if you had maintained your efforts solely on finding referrals and had resisted getting involved in a structured marketing plan. The industry has always promoted two skills. The selling skill was what was needed to convince a prospect to part with his money for your product. It was the "getting skill." The prospecting skill was learning to identify a prospect who had a need you could meet and the ability to pay for it. Now you need a third skill, the ATTRACTION MARKETING SKILL.

> *The selling sales cycle... will become more efficient*

Remember, the attraction marketing skill is learning how to capture "mindshare" before a contact is made. It is different than the prospecting skill. It is all about how to create an Identity Brand where trust becomes established before the contact has been initiated. This is the skill that allows producers to SOAR. It is the skill that makes the competition go away. It is the skill that allows you to claim ownership to a market segment that eventually even the competition must acknowledge is owned by you. Regis McKenna, author of *Relationship Marketing*, writes, "...winning over the customer's mind is the central challenge of marketing." Guy E. Baker, CLU, MSFS in his

> *Regis McKenna, author of Relationship Marketing, "...winning over the customer's mind is the central challenge of marketing."*

book *Why People Buy,* says, "Successful marketing occurs when you are on your client's shelf." (referring to the "shelf of your mind") He goes on to say, "You have succeeded when you are front and center and he thinks of you every time the products and services you represent are mentioned." What can you do to position yourself on the "shelf" of your client's mind? That is what attraction marketing is all about. That is why Guy Baker is one of the top twenty producers in the United States. He understands and works at attraction marketing, not just selling and prospecting.

Maintaining your defined focus becomes much easier once you have your Identity Branding plan formulated. It is all too easy to get trapped into working with the prospect with whom you never should have gotten involved. That continues to occur to those who have only developed selling and prospecting skills and have overlooked marketing. Guy E. Baker, CLU, MSFS says, "What a nice situation to be in, to have a list of pre-qualified prospects who know

> *Guy E. Baker, CLU, MSFS says, "What a nice situation to be in, to have a list of pre-qualified prospects who know what you do, who want to talk to you, and who are accessible because of your marketing skills."*

what you do, who want to talk to you, and who are accessible because of your marketing skills." When you have your market segment individualized, you have a much easier time maintaining your focus. If your intended market were simply identified as "small business owners," would there not be some small business owners with whom you shouldn't work because they are too small or unprofitable? Does every small business owner fit your profile? Even if they did, how can you get on "the shelf of their minds" if you can't individualize them? How can you create "mindshare?" You can't! You must individualize your market to create "mindshare" and to maintain focus on your defined prospect profile.

The final benefit is the strong loyalty you will create within your organization. If you are a sales professional who has support staff, these employees will take on more responsibility and involvement in helping you become Identity Branded than they ever did to help promote your company. Your company is an impersonal object that creates product. Your support staff always saw YOU as the business, but this may be the first time that they clearly see the objective, to promote you as the local brand. They will now see you as the company and they realize that their promotional efforts will reflect not only on your reputation, but also on their prestige within the community. They see this objective as becoming a part of something greater than a "sale professional's staff." They become part of a local market brand.

If you are a manager of an agency, you have an opportunity to utilize your ability to help your sales professionals market their own identity. This creates local identity and differentiation for your agency and becomes your distinction as compared to the competition. This is your advantage. It is not the difference in your company's products as compared to the competition that attracts new hires. The new recruit and administration support people that you hope to hire view all companies as essentially the same. When they see the agency as distinctive, their interest increases. Once hired, they will display pride and loyalty in an agency that is unique. If you want to hire the best people, become known as the best in helping sales professionals become Identity Branded. From this perspective, you will become the most attractive company for which to work.

There are five basic ingredients in Identity Branding. Each step will require some serious thought, but the benefits far outweigh the effort involved.

Five Basic Ingredients For Establishing An Identity Brand

1. **Individualize your targeted market** with specific prospect names and determine to "own" it. Regis McKenna, author of *Relationship Marketing,* says, "When you own the market...you define the standards in that market."

2. **Establish four yearly-specific progress review dates** to evaluate your branding and prospect attraction plan progress. Your structured plan should include all the elements of the diagram shown on the next page.

3. **Create memorable events** that the client and prospect regard as high-value, exceptionally unique, creative and differentiated from the competition. Lynn Upshaw, author of *Building Brand Identity,* says, "A brand's positioning establishes its credibility, but its likability is a direct function of its personality." Frequently give them something to like that has substance.

4. **Consistent Contact** - These two words are critical to the success of your plan and its impact on the prospect. You must provide consistent contact with your audience.

5. **Patience and Persistence** - Give your plan at least one year before critiquing the impact. You will be pleased. Don't stop prematurely or "water down" your plan during the year. The greatest mistakes most agents make are giving up prematurely and not following through.

Your job is to create an Identity Brand that creates a visible distinction, a competitive advantage and answers the question, "Why You?" Once you have accomplished that goal, you will never again have a prospecting problem.

Your job is to create an Identity Brand that...answers the question, "Why You?"

IDENTITY BRANDING

The Prospect Attraction Model (PACC)

Prospect Database
(Social or Belief
Connection)

Consistent Contact
(12 times per year)

Activating Events
(Heighten Awareness for YOU)

**Characteristic
Uniqueness**
(Accentuate Business Differentiation)

The Adventurous Future

You are about to embark on the most exciting challenge you will ever confront. The marketing revolution that is going to grip America will be the stuff from which generational stories are made. It will be like sitting on your great-great-great-grandfather's lap and hearing about the first airplane that he ever saw fly overhead. It will be like seeing the first broadcast TV show or like being present to see a TV show broadcast in color for the first time. However, this change is not about a new revolutionary product being developed and introduced to the public. This change is not just about consumers wanting more information, wanting to be treated more professionally or wanting to know more about the reasoning behind your recommendations. This change is about the consumer having more alternatives than ever before for purchasing anything and everything they may want. It is about the consumer being in control of directing the selling process. It is about the total reversal of how goods are sold, distributed and accessed. The challenge requires a response to meeting the client's demands for what they want, when they want it, where they want it and how they want it.

You have an opportunity to not only survive this change but to prosper from it. Survival is dependent upon your ability to adopt and adapt. Those who delay the process will fail. Speed

Survival is dependent upon your ability to adopt and adapt.

is critical. You will learn by doing, not by cautiously plotting and planning. You will learn by making mistakes. The greatest determining factor necessary for success will be how fast you can recognize your mistakes and recover from them. Resiliency will be key. Quick decisions, coupled with resiliency when errors are made, will be far superior to good decisions that are implemented six months too late.

Lynn Upshaw, author of *Building Brand Identity*, says,

"Interactive communications are here, not in their ultimate form and only a fraction of their ultimate size, but their existence is undeniable, and their future is assured." He goes on to say, "...interactive media offers an advanced form of...relationship marketing" but "Still, there is a real question about how many of today's successful marketers will be able to make the turn into a contemporized selling environment." Electronic communications will play an important role in this marketing revolution and coupling them with building an Identity Brand will be imperative for your business to flourish.

Your effectiveness in getting a sale by demonstrating that your product and service are superior to the competition has diminished, if not totally vanished. A brand is much more than product today. The product you sell is no longer any more singularly defined than McDonald's® defining hamburgers as their business. If McDonald's had defined their business as hamburgers, they would have failed. If they were in hamburger competition, they would come out last. McDonald's attraction is built from the same base that your future needs to be built from, the formulation of a distinct personality, a personal brand created and maintained through activating prospect experiences.

The newly empowered consumers no longer want to listen to the typical sales approach. Just "getting in" to see them is harder. The average person is so squeezed for time today that their tolerance level is as low as it has ever been. They are more hurried, less patient and less tolerant than at any time in

the more distinct your Identity Brand, the greater your chances for success.

history, and it won't get better. The sales professional's survival will be dependent on creating an emotional connection with prospects, before engaging them in even the initial conversation. The "trust sale" will need to have been made before they have met you. The bottom line: the more distinct your Identity Brand, the greater your chances for success.

This next marketing revolution will embrace the new communication technology to maximize the new marketing skills. The two, marketing and technology are no longer adversaries. They are complementary. Both will be key to your future success.

The traffic on this new marketing road is picking up speed. It may appear to be subtle now, but that is about to change. You cannot afford to be lingering on the roadside or yielding to the other traffic. You cannot patiently wait on the ramp for just the right time to enter this new marketing super highway. Yielding to the other traffic will be tantamount to the yield sign reading, "Stop – Give Up All Hope." If you don't pick up speed, you will become a fatality. Determine that this new journey is going to be fun and get into the fast lane. The destination will be better than any other that you have ever witnessed, but the trip is a one-time offering. It is only for those who want to go NOW.

See you there!

IDENTITY BRANDING

Section 5

IDENTITY BRANDING

Keeping On Track

IDENTITY BRANDING

Summary

The approaches in this book are far from exhaustive in giving ways to become unique, distinct and Identity Branded within your local market. However, they point the way to the sort of activities that are required if you are to succeed in the new consumer environment. The challenge for future success does not lie in the traditional selling and prospecting skills of yesterday, nor in the product development department's belief that the "Best" product always rises to the top. Rather, future success lies in the hands of those who focus on attraction marketing, implement meaningful strategies and ultimately answer the consumer's question, "Why you?" before ever meeting them.

Your new focus on attraction marketing won't come naturally, but your successful results will be significant and personally fulfilling. It will be easy to regress, but the consequence of not adapting will eventually prove fatal. It will take effort and concentration to remember that attraction marketing is not about trying to get the sales professional to maintain a positive attitude; it is not about proclaiming a general market definition (i.e., small business market) as your marketing focus and believing that suffices for an attraction marketing plan; it is not about identifying a list of prospect names to target sell; it's not about learning how to close more effectively and it is not about acquiring more advanced training; it's not about print advertising or creating better looking brochures; it's not about service, direct-mail solicitations, telemarketing, Web sites, or trying to do the same things that the competition is doing, but proclaiming that you do them better. *It's about having a known system for identifying your prospect community by individual names and then personally branding YOU - your distinct, unique, intriguing and differentiated Identity Brand into their minds.*

Most companies expect the sales professional to complete technical, continuing education credits each year to stay current. They should also expect them to complete on-going training for attraction marketing. The offices and companies that stay current in attraction marketing, partner in developing local prospect attraction plans and consistently manage and monitor their progress, will retain their people, increase their sales, recruit the new talent that they pursue, increase their profits and have a strategic competitive advantage over the competition.

The letter on the next page, "A Mid-Year Review for Sales Professionals," and the forms that follow may help you self-monitor your own progress as you learn and develop the new skills that the consumer is demanding. Don't get sidetracked. Don't allow attraction marketing to be a secondary focus. Attraction marketing is critical to your future success. Plan your strategy and maintain your persistency. If your strategy is "sound," success will follow.

A Mid-Year Review for Sales Professionals

Dear Sales Professional,

If you have read this book and the majority of your income is determined each year by incentive or commissions, I would encourage you to take a few minutes to read this letter and actively participate when it directs you to highlight or write your comments. This letter is your mid-year "challenge" letter. As a matter of fact, grab a hi-liter NOW and get ready to mark the areas that speak to you personally. This should allow for a self-critique of your understanding and proficiency of the many components within this book and allow you to self-evaluate your potential as compared to your performance so far this year. So, get your hi-liter (I am serious!) and read for about 2 minutes. (GET YOUR HI-LITER OUT NOW instead of deciding after you read that you should have listened and now need to read it again. Got it? OK, now have fun, highlight anything that directly affects you …let's go!)

The first challenge is to be reflective and honest with yourself about your current yearly results. ARE YOU SATISFIED? Use your hi-liter and mark either YES or NO right here. (Did you do it?) We will come back to this question later. (Yes, you can circle one of the answers if you have a pen instead of a high-lighter).

Next, write in the words poor, fair, good or excellent for each of the four areas listed below, indicating what area was most responsible for impeding your desired results. (If you are 100% satisfied with any one area, mark it excellent. If you just didn't get around to seeing enough people, indicate poor after the listing title Prospect/Contact Activity.

For each listing, indicate one of the following: Poor, Fair, Good or Excellent

- Sales or Product Knowledge   _____

- Focus on In-Office Tasks   _____

- Prospect/Contact Activity   _____

- My Prospect Attraction Strategy   _____

Now, write in your desired "performance goal(s)" based on income or prospect contacts that you should attain every month or quarter. This performance goal should be monetary if you are commissioned or on an incentive income program. It may also be a monthly contact goal if you hold yourself responsible for personally opening a certain number of new prospect cases each month.

Goal: _____ per _____ (month or quarter).

Before we go any further with evaluations, take a minute to write down three personal "wants" that you hope to attain in the next twelve months. Remember these are personal wants. Do your best to stay away from items like your company production club or an incentive trip qualification. Make sure that these are material things that cost money, i.e., a new car, new furniture, a two-week vacation, a debt paid off, an amount of money saved or invested by years end. If it's a three-year monetary goal (i.e., saving $50,000 for down payment on a vacation home down payment), just list an amount that is attainable and measurable for the next twelve months. If it's a family cruise for next spring, how much will you save this year or each quarter? While you are listing your three items, imagine really wanting them. Try to feel the emotions you will experience and disappointment that others may have if you don't attain the goal that is needed to meet these "wants." Do you really want to do without? Circle the one most important "want" item, one that you will commit to attaining, and share this with the person in your life who is the most important to you.

Item   Method for measuring progress

1) _____   _____

2) _____   _____

3) _____   _____

(Remember to circle your most important item, the one that you will share!)

Now let's review some BUSINESS ELEMENTS that you should incorporate in order to meet your goals.

1) Do you have a definite, scheduled WEEKLY CHECKPOINT for the one or two priority activities that you must accomplish in order to meet your financial goals? Write down when this occurs, or should occur, and specify what activity you are measuring.

   When is your weekly checkpoint?

   _____

   _____

What are you measuring each week?

_____

_____

2) Identify the market segment(s) around which you want to build your business. How many individualized prospect names can you gather from each segment? What will you do to create a prospect attraction strategy? What ways can you think of to begin effectively networking within this market segment?

Write down the names of your market segments:

a. _____   b. _____

c. _____   d. _____

What is the number of potential names within each segment:

_____

_____

How will you begin your prospect attraction strategy in each segment?

_____

_____

3) How many new names of prospects will you gather each week, month or quarter to add to your *Prospect Fishbowl*? If you don't constantly measure this, eventually you will find yourself working with prospects that don't fit your prospect profile and are below your skill level. You will find yourself wearing out your existing client base, prematurely trying to derive revenue from them and frustrating yourself with your attempts. How many new prospect names will you add?

#_____ per _____

How many total names will you have in your *Prospect Fishbowl* in the next

6 months? _____   12 months? _____

4) How do you consistently familiarize yourself to your prospect audience? How are you creating a visible attraction that identifies you as distinctly unique within your market segment? Be specific:

_____

_____

5) What do you need to do to build an alliance with a complementary organization, such as a CPA or P&C Firm? Who will it be? What should be your first step? When will you take it?

_____

_____

6) What do you need to do to merge communication technology with relationship building? What technology plans are you pursuing in order to communicate with your clients and prospects in the future so that you meet their expectations?

_____

_____

7) Determine to make an appointment every week, every two weeks or monthly with a new prospect, whose level of sophistication requires a joint-work effort with a more experienced associate or a specialist in your office. Determine to work "over your head" on a predetermined scheduled basis. You will increase your ability by leaps and bounds. Even if you are the experienced associate, let someone else carry the case that is beyond your skill level while you watch. Set a schedule for just one joint-work effort on a regular basis and honor it! Write down how often you will do this and what kind of reminder you will give yourself so that it doesn't get forgotten.

_____

_____

8) Commit to completing a courageous act every day before 10:00 a.m. A courageous act might be making that call to someone by whom you are intimidated. Maybe it is calling on a business owner for an appointment or contacting someone that you know from civic club but have never called on. The item changes every day and week, but a courageous act must

always be a revenue producing activity. Signing up for a compliance exam or cleaning the paperwork off your desk does not qualify. A courageous act is about doing "scary" things that are easy to put off and always seem worse before you face them than after they are completed. No one becomes successful without tackling "scary" issues. The better you are, the more successful you become. And remember, do one act by 10:00 a.m. each day. How will you track your "courageous acts"? Make a special place each day in your day timer?

Write your courageous act focus! _____

_____

_____

9) Develop a habit of recording those items that you would consider VICTORIES at the end of each week. Maybe it was calling on a prospect that you had feared and it successfully resulted in an appointment. Maybe it was setting up a referral or endorsement luncheon that ended up quite successful. Maybe it was deciding to close a case with a client who had been stalling, for no apparent reason, and your efforts paid off. If you have young children, consider doing this as a family project with your kids. Establish a consistent time with your family, at a meal or at bedtime on Friday night after the week is over. Label a small notebook "MY VICTORY LOG" and record their victories. You won't believe the increase in confidence this new reality will provide. It will become your children's favorite book...and yours. You are building new levels of confidence and pride. It is not based on hype. It is who you are. It is based on all the victories that we so easily forget; the victories we allow to become overshadowed by even the smallest setbacks. It's recognizing and giving

yourself credit for the reality of how good you are. It is the main element for building self-esteem. Imagine the impact this would have on your children. How will you implement this? (Do it with your children.)

_____

_____

Ok, this concludes your year-to-date challenge and self-evaluation. The ideas that you have written down will help to propel your future success. The future is going to be different and to succeed, you, too, will have to change. Old methods and strategies will no longer work. Even working harder will not suffice this time. You will need to look and be different from the competition. You will need to have a more directed focus. You will have to have a familiarization plan that identifies you to your market segment prospects before you call on them. You will need to make an impact, not at the time of your first meeting, but far in advance of it. You will need to become an effective entrepreneur who builds a business on an attraction marketing model instead of on a selling model. For those who are successful, the future will be bright. Your success is dependent on becoming DISTINCT...and if you don't, you can expect to become EXTINCT. It's entirely up to you.

Best wishes for a bright future,

Robert E Krumroy
President
Identity Branding, Inc.

Ten Challenge Questions
for Refocusing To A Market Segment

> "Never get so involved in your work that you neglect to keep those important marketing and public relations activities going. Your target market needs to hear from you regularly in your public relationship and marketing activities." William J. Bond, *Going Solo,* (NY, NY: McGraw-Hill, 1997)

1) What privileged service do my *A clients (top 20%)* receive?

_____

_____

What should I add to intensify these relationships?

_____

_____

2) How do my *A clients* know that they are a select class? What special event / function / service do I provide for them?

_____

_____

IDENTITY BRANDING

3) What do I expect from my *A clients* in return for what I extend to them?

_____

_____

How have I related this expectation to them?

_____

_____

4) How do I avoid personal involvement in my *B client* and *C client* service needs, yet make sure that their needs are being met (i.e., customer service rep, etc.)?

_____

_____

5) What market segment(s) of prospects (not clients) do I consistently communicate with using a specific contact strategy?

_____

_____

What *should* I be doing?

_____

_____

6) What unique and differentiated events am I implementing or participating in to accentuate my emotional connection with my prospect market(s)?

_____

_____

7) What specific attraction-marketing activities will I conduct in the next twelve months to place me in front of significant groups of prospects within my market segment(s)?

_____

_____

How many unique attraction-marketing events will I conduct per year?

_____

_____

8) How many prospects, that meet my prospect profile, will I add to my *Prospect Fishbowl* this year? _____

What will my total number of prospects be in my database at year-end? _____

9) What consistent contact method will I use to capture "mindshare" of my clients and prospects within my *Prospect Fishbowl?*

_____

_____

How often? _____

10) What new things should I be doing that will make the greatest positive impact to my reputation and my accessibility to my market segment(s) in the next 5 years?

_____

_____

Methods for Cultivating Your "A" Clientele

1) Take one "A" client to lunch every week and tell them they are special and appreciated.

2) Send flowers or birthday cakes (delivered personally to your "A" clients on their birthdays). What will I do?

_____

_____

3) Have a yearly "A" client appreciation event (Top 25). The mingling opportunity will cause numerous new sales opportunities to surface.

4) Meet with every A *client* at least 2 times per year over lunch.

5) Get to know every A *client* on a a personal basis. Build your personal information in your database. Send an article of personal interest once or twice a year to each A client. How will I do this?

_____

_____

6) Send an e-Financial Storyboard eight times per year continuing to accentuate the areas you specialize in. Watch the new cross-selling opportunities increase. Comments:

_____

_____

7) Be punctual. Do what you promise.

References and Acknowledgements

1) Baker, Guy E. *(Why People Buy)* (Standel Publishing, 1995)
2) Baron, Gerald R. *(Friendship Marketing)* (Grants Pass, Oregon: The Oasis Press, 1997)
3) Beckwith, Harry *(Selling The Invisible)* (New York, NY: Warner Books, Inc., 1997)
4) Bond, William J. *(Going Solo)* (New York, NY: McGraw-Hill, 1997)
5) Boylan, Michael *(The Power To Get In)* (New York, NY: St. Martin's Press, 1997)
6) Clancey, Kevin J. and Robert S. Shulman *(Marketing Myths That are Killing Business)* (New York, NY: McGraw-Hill, 1995)
7) Conlon, Ginger, *"No Turning Back,"* Sales and Marketing Management, December 1999, PP. 50-52, 54, 55.
8) Dale, Wally *(Collaborative Database Marketing)* (Washington, DC: GAMA Foundation, 1999)
9) Debelak, Don *(Marketing Magic)* (Adams Media Corp; 1997)
10) Gregory, James R. and Jack G. Wiechmann *(Marketing Corporate Image)* (Chicago: NTC Business Books, 1999)
11) Harding, Ford *(Creating Rainmakers)* (Holbrook, MA: Adams Media Corporation, 1998)
12) Hiebing, Jr., Roman and Scott W. Cooper *(The One-Day Marketing Plan)* (Chicago: NTC Publishing Group, 1999)
13) Ingari, Frank *"The Internet as a Marketing Medium,"* Strategy and Business, Fourth Quarter 1999, PP. 6-8.
14) Kawasaki, Guy *(Selling The Dream)* (New York, NY: Harper Collins Publishers, 1991)
15) Kennedy, Dan *(The Ultimate Marketing Plan)* (Holbrook, MA: Adams Media Corporation, 1991)
16) Lenzner, Robert and Ashlea Ebeling *"A Wealth of Names – David Rockefeller Sr. is The Ultimate Rainmaker,"* Forbes, January 10, 2000, PP. 70, 71.
17) Levitt, Theodore *(The Marketing Imagination)* (New York, NY: The Free Press, 1986)
18) McKenna, Regis *(Real Time)* (Harvard Business School Press, 1999)
19) McKenna, Regis *(Relationship Marketing)* (Reading, MA: Addison-Wesley, 1998)
20) Misner, Ph. D., Ivan and Virginia Divine *(The Worlds Best Known Marketing Secret)* (Austin, Texas: Bard Press, 1999)
21) Palmer, Parker *(Let Your Life Speak)* (San Francisco, California: Jossey-Bass publishers, 2000)
22) Pritchett, Price *(New Work Habits For a Radically Changing World)* (Dallas, Texas: Pritchett & Associates, Incorporated, 1998)
23) Prince, Russ and Karen File *(Marketing Through Advisors)* (Cincinnati, Ohio: National Underwriter, 1996)
24) Ries, Al and Jack Trout *(Positioning – The Battle For Your Mind)* (New York, NY: Warner Books and McGraw-Hill, 1986)
25) Schmitt, Bernd H. *(Experiential Marketing)* (Free Press, 1999)
26) Stanley, Dr. Thomas *(Networking With The Affluent)* (New York, NY: McGraw-Hill, 1993)
27) Sullivan, Dan *(The 21st Century Agent)* (Toronto, Canada: The Strategic Coach Inc., 1995)
28) Upshaw, Lynn *(Building Brand Identity)* (John Wiley & Sons, Inc., 1995)

IDENTITY BRANDING

About the Author

Robert E. Krumroy, CLU, ChFC, is president of Identity Branding, Inc., an organization devoted to assisting the financial sales professional in creating distinct and unique local market prospect attraction. The result is a perception of superior value and market separation, both of which give the agent a local competitive advantage and solves the issue of "market access." Krumroy began his career as an insurance agent, transitioned into management and was recognized nationally as a sixteen-time National Management qualifier and one of the very few national Master-Agency Award qualifiers in the financial services industry. He is a featured columnist, a frequent article contributor to magazines, has served on the GAMA teaching faculty for "Best Practices" and is a highly sought after speaker. He has been introduced on many occasions as the most brilliant marketing mind in the financial services industry and has been a main platform presenter at most of the industry conventions, nationally and internationally. .

As an attraction-marketing consultant, author, columnist, speaker and "Branding Workshop" leader, he provides a wide range of resources for business, educational organizations and individuals including:

• Keynote Presentations

• Attraction Marketing Workshops (half-days)

• Comprehensive "Prospect Attraction Plan" Manuals

• Strategic Identity Branding Consulting for National Companies

• Building a Brand Culture for Local Offices (half-day)

• E-Relationship™ Rollout Meetings

For more information on the wide range of resources available from Robert Krumroy, visit our Web site at:

www.identitybranding.com

www.e-relationship.com

or just call, email, write or fax:

Identity Branding, Inc.
2007 Yanceyville Street, Box 2
Greensboro, NC 27405

Toll free: 1-800-851-8169
Fax: 1-336-303-7318
E-mail: info@identitybranding.com